WEBSTER'S UNIVERSAL
COMPUTER DICTIONARY

WEBSTER'S UNIVERSAL
COMPUTER DICTIONARY

GEDDES & GROSSET

Published 2007 by Geddes & Grosset,
David Dale House,
New Lanark, ML11 9DJ, Scotland

Copyright © 1998, 2004 Geddes & Grosset

Original text by Keith White, 1998
Additional text and revision by Richard Bowen, 2004

All rights reserved. No part of this publication may be reproduced, stored in a retrieval system, or transmitted, in any form or by any means, electronic, mechanical, photocopying, recording or otherwise without the prior permission of the copyright holder

ISBN 978 1 84205 634 9

Printed and bound in India

A

@
The "at" part of an EMAIL/Internet ADDRESS, which separates a user name from a DOMAIN NAME.

abort
To cancel or terminate a process or procedure while it is in progress.

absolute link
A HYPERLINK that specifies the full PATH to a TARGET file, where the ROOT DIRECTORY is taken as the highest possible LEVEL within a system, i.e. the working DISK, or the INTERNET ADDRESS. In the case of the latter, an absolute link is also the URL, e.g. http://www.google.com/. If changes are made to the local DIRECTORY STRUCTURE, an absolute link will become a BROKEN LINK.

accelerated graphics port
see AGP.

accelerator board
An adapter for the computer containing a more advanced microprocessor than the one already in the computer. Adding an accelerator can speed up the computer generally or can speed up a particular function, such as the graphics display.

access
To locate and retrieve the information, whether in the

access code

form of data or PROGRAM instructions, stored on a disk or in a computer; *access time* refers to the amount of time it takes to transfer information from one source to another. It is measured in nanoseconds (ns) for memory chips and in milliseconds (ms) for data transfer from the hard disk. The access time is determined by the time required for the disk heads to move to the correct track (the seek time), and then to settle down (the settle time) and the time needed for the sector to move under the head (latency).

access code
The means of gaining entry into a computer or system by use of a password or specific identification number.

access point
A BASE STATION for WIRELESS NETWORK users to connect to a LAN. Access points work in a way that is similar to a cellular phone network. Each point has a range of several hundred feet, and users are automatically handed from one to another as they move around. When this is applied to the public provision of wireless access to a network, e.g. at a railroad station or airport, an access point is known as a HOTSPOT. *See also* MOBILE INTERNET; WAP.

access provider
A company that provides connections to the Internet. Such companies are known as an INTERNET ACCESS PROVIDER, or INTERNET SERVICE PROVIDER.

accessibility
WEB DESIGN can present barriers to people with

disabilities, especially people with sensory or neurological disabilities. Accessibility refers to the ease with which a user with an impairment can utilize a WEB PAGE (or application). There are various items of HARDWARE and SOFTWARE that help people who are impaired, but the first step is in the design of the WEBSITE itself. The key reference point for accessibility issues is the WEB ACCESSIBILITY INITIATIVE.

acoustic coupler
A unit that comprises a cradle to hold a telephone handset and a modem. Such devices have been superseded by modems integrated in computers and mobile phones.

Acrobat Reader
see ADOBE ACROBAT.

acronym
The abbreviation of words to their initial letters to enable more rapid communication; often used in Internet CHAT and TEXT MESSAGING, or DIGISPEAK.

active cell
The CELL in a SPREADSHEET in which the CURSOR is currently positioned, allowing a number or FORMULA to be entered.

active matrix display
A LIQUID CRYSTAL DISPLAY in which each of the display's electrodes is under the control of it's own transistor. Active matrix displays are more expensive than a lower resolution PASSIVE MATRIX DISPLAY.

active window

active window
In an APPLICATION or OPERATING SYSTEM that can display multiple windows, the active WINDOW is the one that accepts commands or typing and is indicated by a colored bar at the top of the window.

Active X®
A technology developed by MICROSOFT that is mainly used for EMBEDDING executable content in a WEB PAGE, such as a spreadsheet, and which therefore has a similar aim as an APPLET. The executable CODE is known as an *ActiveX control*, and controls come with a DIGITAL CERTIFICATE.

Ada
A programming language developed around 1980.

adapter card
A CARD complete with electronic components that plugs into the computer's main CIRCUIT BOARD with the aim of providing enhanced capabilities. Adapter cards can be used to provide high quality graphics, modems, etc.

ADb
see APPLE DESKTOP BUS.

ADC (Analog to Digital Converter)
see DIGITAL CAMERA.

add in program
A small PROGRAM that is designed to complement an APPLICATION and add to the capabilities of the host application.

Adobe Acrobat

address
A location in a computer system that is identified by a name or code. The address is specified by the PROGRAM or the user. It is also a line of words and/or numbers that identifies an EMAIL or INTERNET location.

A person's email address consists of their name, number, abbreviated name, initials, etc. followed by the @ symbol and then the SERVER through whom mail is sent, and from whom mail is collected.

address book
A useful facility within the PROGRAM for EMAIL which enables the user to record email addresses.

address bus
An electronic channel linking the MICROPROCESSOR to the random access memory (*see* RAM) along which the addresses of MEMORY locations are transmitted.

Adobe Acrobat
Highly popular and successful DOCUMENT EXCHANGE SOFTWARE. Acrobat converts documents from most applications into a PORTABLE DOCUMENT FORMAT file, which is a stable format that can then be viewed on any other computer that has the READER software installed.

Formerly known as *Acrobat Reader*, Adobe Reader is available free from the Adobe website. Acrobat gets around FONT INCOMPATIBILITY in two ways – it has its own list of integral fonts, with which it can carry out FONT SUBSTITUTION, or it can embed the fonts form the original. *See* EMBEDDING.

Adobe Type Manager (ATM)

Adobe Type Manager (ATM)
A POSTSCRIPT utility for MACINTOSH and WINDOWS, allowing PostScript fonts to be viewed properly on-screen, and to be printed to non-PostScript printers, by sending a bitmapped image of the fonts to the printer. *See also* BITMAP; RASTER; RIP.

ADSL (Asymmetrical Digital Subscriber Line)
A fast asymmetric communication technology that is ideal for consumer connection to the INTERNET, as it allows more DATA to be transmitted quickly over existing telephone lines. ADSL supports data receiving speeds of 1.5 to 9 Mbps (the DOWNSTREAM RATE) and 16 to 640 Kbps when sending (the UPSTREAM RATE), which is why it is termed asymmetric. Compare to an ISDN rate of 128 Kbps.

A special MODEM is required, as well as having a compatible telephone service and a specific user subscription. Prices are decreasing with rapidly growing popularity, and, increasingly, a choice of speeds is available. *See also* BROADBAND.

affiliate program
An agreement between one WEBSITE owner and another, whereby one pays the other for every visitor who has come from the other site. Pioneers of such programs include companies like Amazon. Payments are either made as commission on a sale, or per visitor. Being an affiliate entails placing a HYPERLINK prominently on a WEB PAGE, or adding an interface of some sort, usually supplied by the other owner. The success of the market has spawned various trading intermediary businesses, who deal with processing the commissions. Also known as *associate programs*.

agent
A PROGRAM that helps to carry out a task, e.g. a diary reminder. There are various different types of agent. *Reactive agents* simply make a response, e.g. an email alert. *Deliberative agents* can carry out quite complicated tasks, e.g. a software "helper". *Collaborative agents* work together, e.g. a diary agent could collaborate with an agent used for booking tickets. An agent is very similar to a BOT.

aGP (Accelerated Graphics Port)
A high-speed graphics PORT developed by Intel and based on PCI, but designed specially for the processing of 3-D GRAPHICS. It provides a dedicated connection between the display ADAPTER CARD and main memory. AGP was introduced as a high-speed alternative to the PCI-based adapter. *See also* ACCELERATOR BOARD; TEXTURE MAPPING.

AI
see ARTIFICIAL INTELLIGENCE.

AIFF (Audio Interchange File Format)
An audio file FORMAT used on the MACINTOSH. It breaks the file into chunks - the Common chunk holds file information, such as the SAMPLING rate; the Sound Data chunk contains the sound itself.

AIX (Advanced Interactive eXecutive)
A variant of the UNIX operating system developed by IBM primarily for their workstations.

alert box
A WINDOW appearing on a SCREEN providing a warning

algorithm
that an error has occurred or the COMMAND chosen may result in lost work.

algorithm
A set of straightforward logical mathematical steps that, if followed, provide a solution to a problem.

alias
A representation of an original DOCUMENT or FILE that can be used as if it was the original. An alias's name appears in italics. An alias is not a copy of the file but a small file that directs the computer to the original file. Using an alias can assist in file storage and retrieval.

aliasing
see JAGGIES.

alignment
see READ/WRITE HEAD ALIGNMENT; TEXT ALIGNMENT.

alphanumeric character
Any KEYBOARD character that can be typed, such as: A to Z in either uppercase or lowercase, numbers 1 to 10 and punctuation marks.

analog
The opposite of DIGITAL. An analog signal varies continuously to reflect the changes in the state of the quantity being measured, e.g. sound waves vary continually. A thermometer is an analog measurement device, and as the temperature varies so does the height of the mercury. On the other hand, digital signals are either on or off.

AND
see FORMULA; LOGICAL OPERATOR.

animation
A GRAPHIC creation that gives the impression of movement by showing a series of slides on the computer SCREEN. Each slide is slightly different from the previous slide and when the images are played back fast enough, the movement appears smooth.

anonymous FTP
see FTP.

ANSI (American National Standards Institute)
A non-governmental organization founded in 1981 to approve the specification of DATA PROCESSING standards in the USA. It is also responsible for the definition of high-level programming languages.

anti-aliasing
The process whereby the jagged appearance of a sloping line is made smooth. A bit-mapped image is made up of pixels that, especially at higher magnification, can be seen as filled-in boxes. Anti-aliasing changes some of the fringe boxes to shades of gray or a color to create a smoother appearance to the line edge. When applied to color this is called dithering (*see* DITHER and JAGGIES).

anti-virus program
A program that checks the COMPUTER for and protects it from VIRUSES. Viruses are identified either by the presence of virus codes or by effects such as corrupted files.

AOL (America OnLine)

AOL (America OnLine)
AOL is the world's biggest ONLINE INFORMATION SERVICE and INTERNET SERVICE PROVIDER and provides users with a comprehensive online experience, particularly geared towards family and child use.

AOL acquired COMPUSERVE in the 1990s, and also bought up Netscape, the developer of the only large-scale competitor to Microsoft's INTERNET EXPLORER. AOL has since "merged" with Time Warner.

AOL Instant Messenger (AIM) is a very popular INSTANT MESSAGING SERVICE available to all Internet users for free.

API
see APPLICATION PROGRAM INTERFACE.

APL (A Program Language)
A HIGH-LEVEL PROGRAMMING LANGUAGE designed for handling engineering and mathematical functions and as a notation for communication between mathematicians. It is quick and efficient.

Apple Computer Inc.
A pioneering company based in California, which develops, manufactures, licenses and markets products, technologies and services for consumers in over 140 countries. The brand name of its range of computers is MACINTOSH®.

Apple Desktop bus (ADb)
A standard INTERFACE for Apple computers that allows connection of input devices such as keyboards, mice, graphics tablets and trackballs to all MACINTOSH computers. Up to 16 ADb devices can be connected to

the computer, which can receive data at approximately 4.5 kilobits (i.e. 4500 bits) per second.

AppleShare
A NETWORK OPERATING SYSTEM that converts an Apple MACINTOSH computer into a FILE SERVER for a NETWORK. The server can be accessed by the network as if it were an added HARD DISK.

Applet
A minor APPLICATION or PROGRAM that runs within another application. Applets are commonly written using JAVA language and can be found on the INTERNET. They are CROSS-PLATFORM, and can be used on WINDOWS, MACINTOSH and UNIX computers, providing the host machine has the appropriate software.

AppleTalk
A program that connects computers and other HARDWARE such as printers together in a LOCAL AREA NETWORK. Every Apple computer has AppleTalk network facilities built in.

application
A computer PROGRAM that performs specific tasks such as letter writing, statistical analysis, design, etc. Applications work with the OPERATING SYSTEM to control PERIPHERAL devices such as printers.

application program interface (API)
A set of ROUTINES, PROTOCOLS, and TOOLS for building APPLICATIONS. Most OPERATING SYSTEMS provide an API so that programmers can write applications consistent with

Archie (ARCHIvE)

the system. APIs ensure that all programs using a common API will have a similar interface. This makes it easier to learn new programs.

Archie (ARCHIvE)

An Internet UTILITY for FILE NAME searching. There are quite a few systems on the Internet, called Archie servers, that maintain catalogs of files available for downloading. Archie servers search FTP sites and record information about the files that they locate.

archive

A store of files (either PROGRAM or DATA) that is kept as a BACKUP in case the original files are corrupted or damaged. An archived file is often stored in a compressed format (*see* COMPRESS) in order to use up less disk space.

arithmetic operator

A symbol that indicates which arithmetical operation to perform. In a SPREADSHEET, arithmetic operators are used to compile formulae for adding (+), subtracting (−), multiplying (*) or dividing (/) the contents of cells to obtain the desired result.

array

A form in which DATA is stored by computer programs. An array is a table of data. The data is accessed by naming the array and then by the X and Y coordinates.

artificial intelligence (AI)

The ability of an artificial mechanism to exhibit intelligent behavior by modifying its actions through reasoning and learning from experience. Artificial intelligence is also the name of the research discipline in which artificial mechanisms that exhibit intelligence are developed and studied.

ascending order
A method of sorting DATA in a list with the result that the data is arranged from 1 to 10 or A to Z. DESCENDING ORDER reverses the sort order.

ASCII (American Standard Code for Information Interchange)
One of several standard sets of codes devised in 1968 that define the way information is transferred from one COMPUTER to another. It is one method of representing BINARY code, whereby specific binary patterns are represented by alphanumeric characters. The standard ASCII code contains 96 upper and lower case characters and 32 control characters that are not displayed.

ASCII file
Such a FILE is composed entirely of ASCII characters. ASCII files facilitate transfer of DATA when no other file FORMAT will work. A TEXT FILE is often the same as an ASCII file.

assembly language
A LOW-LEVEL PROGRAMMING LANGUAGE that is based on instructions that relate directly to the processing CHIP. (*See also* HIGH-LEVEL PROGRAMMING LANGUAGE.)

Assistant
A series of steps in an APPLICATION, similar to a WIZARD,

asymmetrical digital subscriber line

that assists the user to create a particular DOCUMENT style such as mailing lists, advertising flyers, newsletters, envelopes, etc.

asymmetrical digital subscriber line
see ADSL.

asynchronous communication
A commonly-used mode of transmitting DATA over telephone lines. The two communicating systems are not synchronized – the sending of a character is not dependent on when a previous character is sent or received.

Asynchronous Transfer Mode (ATM)
A NETWORK technology that uses ASYNCHRONOUS COMMUNICATION. An ATM network is structured much like a WIDE AREA NETWORK. ATM is both flexible and fast – it can handle DATA sent at either a constant or variable rate, and is extremely fast. ATM is also capable of being used for LOCAL AREA NETWORKS. *See also* B-ISDN.

ATM
see ADOBE TYPE MANAGER; ASYNCHRONOUS TRANSFER MODE

attachment
(*see also* BINARY FILE) a FILE attached to an EMAIL. It may be in an EPS, TIFF or similar format, a SPREADSHEET, WORD PROCESSING, or DESKTOP PUBLISHING file, or a scanned image. Standard communications are in plain ASCII text so when attachments are also sent, a special encoding program processes the file. For this to work successfully, the recipient's COMPUTER has to have the same set-up.

autoexec.bat

In general, this is the case and a common method in use is MIME. Compression of files reduces the time it takes to DOWNLOAD them; graphics, for example, can be sent as JPEGs.

attribute
in DOS, a classification that determines how a FILE is handled. A file attribute can be: READ/WRITE, READ ONLY, archive, hidden.
In documents, a characteristic that changes how an image, or some text, or other OBJECT is displayed, e.g. bold font. Similarly, in HTML, a TAG is modified by the use of an attribute.

AutoCAD
A widely used but very expensive CAD program.

auto-dial
A feature of most communications programs in which the PROGRAM automatically dials the appropriate phone number and makes a connection with the answering COMPUTER.

auto-dial/auto-answer modem
A MODEM that is able to generate tones to dial the receiving COMPUTER and also to answer the telephone and establish a link when a call is received.

autoexec.bat
The batch file that DOS automatically executes when *booting up*, containing commands that are always executed at the beginning of a session, e.g. launching a MEMORY-RESIDENT PROGRAM. These days, such commands

auto-responder

tend to be located in the WINDOWS system and INITIALISATION files. *See* BOOT.

auto-responder
A means whereby a message can automatically be sent to the email ADDRESS of anyone sending a simple EMAIL message. This is a useful tool for any company that wants to deal with requests for product information, price lists, etc.

auto-save
A UTILITY that regularly saves the work being done on a COMPUTER onto the HARD DISK. It is important to save work regularly otherwise there is a risk of loss of work because of, for example, a power or computer failure. The auto-save utility sets the computer to save at specific intervals, allowing the user to progress with productive work.

auxiliary storage
Another term for SECONDARY STORAGE.

avatar
An ICON that represents the user within a VIRTUAL REALITY environment. Generally, if an avatar is offered, you have a number of choices regarding appearance. Some advanced examples are animated. A great deal of this terminology and iconography derives from "sword and sorcery" gaming.

B

BABT (British Approvals Board for Telecommunications)
An organization that approves all devices for use with the public telephone network, e.g. modems, FAX cards and servers (not acoustic couplers).

back office
refers to the parts of a commercial NETWORK that assist and control business supply and support. Also the SOFTWARE that does this. Areas of business such applications cover include planning, inventory, manufacturing, and all of the activities associated with procurement, services and supply. Where customers can interact with the organization electronically, the systems need to provide a FRONT OFFICE, too. *See also* CLIENT/SERVER.

backbone
The main "trunk route" of the pathways that carry TRAFFIC, i.e. information, on the NET. The highest speeds of transmission operate on the backbone, and smaller networks are connected to it.

background task
Some operating systems allow more than one task to be completed at a time. The main or high priority procedure is carried out in the foreground and lower priority procedures are carried out in the background (*see also* FOREGROUND TASK).

backlit screen

backlit screen
A type of DISPLAY mostly used in NOTEBOOK or LAPTOP COMPUTERS. The display uses LCD technology to light the display behind the text. The text is contrasted against the background.

backslash
in DOS/WINDOWS, this character (\) represents the ROOT DIRECTORY and is also used to separate items in a PATH, each slash representing a step in the DIRECTORY STRUCTURE. HTML uses the forward slash (/), while MACINTOSH uses the colon (:).

backspace
A KEYBOARD key that moves the CURSOR to the left, deleting any previously typed characters.

backup
A copy of a PROGRAM or DATA FILE that is kept for ARCHIVE purposes, usually on a removable or external DISK or DRIVE.

backup utility
An easy-to-use PROGRAM that automatically makes a copy of the main storage DISK of a COMPUTER. The copy or backup is usually made onto TAPE, OPTICAL DISK or FLOPPY DISK.

backward compatible
To be COMPATIBLE with earlier versions of the same product; able to use DATA created by an older version. A computer model is backward compatible if it can run the same SOFTWARE as the previous one.

Until recently, manufacturers have tried hard to keep

barcode

all their products backward compatible. However, technological development has tended to require the sacrifice of compatibility at some point. For instance, WINDOWS XP and MACINTOSH OS X.

It should also be noted that building backward compatibility into software tends to result in very large and memory-hungry applications..

See also UPWARD COMPATIBILE; COMPATIBLE.

bad sector

A part of a disk (HARD DISK or FLOPPY DISK) that cannot be used to record DATA. Bad sectors can be generated in manufacturing, caused by damage in handling the disk or by dust. When a bad sector is identified, the disk should be discarded if it is a floppy, or reformatted if it is a hard disk.

bandwidth

A measure of the range of frequencies that can pass through an INTEGRATED CIRCUIT. The greater the bandwidth the more information that can pass through the circuit.

banner ad

common on the NET, these adverts are elongated rectangles occupying all or most of the width of the page in view .

barcode

A series of printed vertical bars of differing widths that represent numbers. Barcodes identify products for stock control and sales pricing, and can be read by appropriate software.

base station

base station
A transceiving station for WIRELESS NETWORK ACCESS POINTS, cellular phones, pagers and other wireless communication systems.

BASIC (Beginner's All-purpose Symbolic Instruction Code)
one of the most popular computer programming languages. It was developed at Dartmouth College in the USA in 1964 by John Kemeny and Thomas Kurtz. BASIC is available on a wide range of computer platforms and is one of the easiest languages in which to program. It is normally an interpretative LANGUAGE, with each statement being interpreted and executed as it is encountered. It can also be a compiled language, with all the statements being compiled into MACHINE CODE before execution. Early versions of BASIC were criticized for not encouraging structured programming. New versions of BASIC, i.e. Visual Basic, are very powerful indeed.

BAT
The common extension used at the end of a BATCH FILE name.

batch file
A FILE containing DOS commands that is accessed by typing the file name at the DOS prompt. This file type has the extension .BAT.

batch processing
A type of computer operation that processes a series or batch of commands at one time without user

intervention. A BATCH FILE, for example, processes a group of DOS commands on start-up to assist the user.

Baud
A measure of telecommunications transmission speed denoting the number of discrete signal elements that can be transmitted per second. Devised by a 19th-century French telecommunications pioneer, JM Baudot, the *baud rate* is the standard way of representing information in telex and telegraph communications. It commonly refers to the changes in signal frequency per second, and not BITS per second (unless at low baud rates (300), where it is equal to bits per second). At higher rates, the number of bits per second transmitted is higher than the baud rate, and one change in the electrical state of the circuit represents more than one bit of data. This means that 1200 bits per second can be sent at 600 baud.

BBS
see BULLETIN BOARD SERVICE

bells and whistles
The advanced features that an APPLICATION contains.

benchmark
A measurement standard used to compare the performance of different computers and equipment. Standard measures of processor speeds (*see* CLOCK SPEED) do not take account of the speed of other devices such as disk drives or communications, whereas modern benchmark tests take all factors of the COMPUTER SYSTEM into account.

Bernoulli

Bernoulli
A type of DISK DRIVE, usually holding over 20 megabytes of DATA, that uses removable cartridges.

Beta software
The final pre-release version of a piece of SOFTWARE, which is distributed for testing to a standing community of Beta testers, usually experienced volunteers.

Beta testing
The final stage of testing of a computer PROGRAM before it is released for general sale. The testing is usually performed by a number of selected users who have knowledge of, and skill in, using the particular type of APPLICATION.

Bezier curve
A style of curve that depends on vector forces of power and angle to determine its shape. In computer GRAPHICS these curves are manipulated by control handles at the midpoints of a curve.

bidirectional
A term to describe to describe the capability to both transmit and receive data, often used in reference to computer ports and cables. There are bidirectional printer ports, and SERIAL cables are bidirectional. (*See also* PORT; PARALLEL PORT; SERIAL COMMUNICATION; EPP.)

Big Blue
The colloquial name given to IBM (International Business Machines Corporation), one of the largest

computer companies in the world. Blue is the company's corporate color.

binary
The language of all computers, in which all numbers, letters and special characters are represented by 1 and 0. It is called "base two notation". (*See* BINARY NUMBERS.)

binary digit
see BIT.

binary file
The vast majority of files used on a COMPUTER are binary files – formatted word processing files, databases and spreadsheets, graphics, sounds, patches, etc. This means that all the available bits (eight) of information in the BYTE are used. ASCII text differs in that it requires only seven bits and this simpler form is the basis for simple text files in all systems. (*See also* ATTACHMENT).

binary numbers
The use of a base notation of two compared with a base notation of 10 in decimal numbers and 16 in a HEXADECIMAL numbering system. In base two, there are only two digits, 0 or 1. This can then represent the switching on or off of an electric current, thus making it possible to tell an electronic calculating machine, or COMPUTER, what to do.

biometrics
The study of measurable biological characteristics, (which, with reference to computer security systems, includes facial characteristics; iris and retinal patterns,

hand geometry, fingerprints, speech recognition and graphology) in order to establish and verify identity. Biometrics are a more secure form of authentication than PASSWORDS or even SMART CARDS, and are being adopted increasingly by governments for the purposes of anti-terrorism protection. Many believe that biometrics will play a large role in future personal computing. *See also* SPEECH RECOGNITION.

BIOS (Basic Input Output System)
This is a set of programs that is located on a CHIP in the ROM. It provides a link between the OPERATING SYSTEM and the PERIPHERAL hardware, i.e. allows transfer of DATA and commands between the SYSTEM and the HARDWARE, such as displays, disk drives and keyboards. The BIOS also supports the REAL-TIME CLOCK, which provides the date and time each occasion the computer is switched on.

B-ISDN (Broadband Integrated Services Digital Network)
A NETWORK technology which provides sufficient BANDWIDTH to allow the use of applications that were previously impracticable, such as video STREAMING. B-ISDN utilizes an ASYNCHRONOUS COMMUNICATION technology known as ASYNCHRONOUS TRANSFER MODE. See also ISDN; BROADBAND.

bit
The smallest unit of information in a digital COMPUTER. It has a value of 0 or 1 that represents yes/no and either/or choices. A collection of eight bits is called a BYTE. (*See also* BINARY NUMBERS.)

bitmap

A method of storing GRAPHICS information in MEMORY, in which a BIT is devoted to each PIXEL on SCREEN. A bitmap contains a bit for each point or dot on a VIDEO DISPLAY, and can allow for fine RESOLUTION because each point on the display can be addressed. A *bit-mapped font* is a FONT for screen and/or PRINTER in which every CHARACTER is made up of a pattern of dots. To allow display or printing, a full record must be kept in the computer's memory.

bitmapped graphics

see PAINT PROGRAM.

bits per second

see BPS.

block

A selection of information that can be dealt with by one series of commands. For example, in SPREADSHEET applications a block of information can be selected and copied to another part of the sheet.

blog

Abbreviation of WEBLOG. A WEB PAGE serving as a personal journal or covering a subject of interest to the author. It is, however, designed to be freely available to other Internet users and is regularly updated (known as *blogging*). Blogs naturally tend to reflect the personality of the author and are a little like a cross between publishing your own diary and a specialist magazine or fanzine.

Blogs often contain LINKS to other sites of interest or

blogger

relevance. There is usually a summary of the referenced sites, along with commentary. Blogs have become very popular, enabling a BLOGGER to publish information about any subject, even if only their day-to-day life. The blogger community at large is known as the *blogosphere*. There are websites that provide tools for creating blogs, e.g. templates, and which will host your blog and optimize your connectivity with the blogosphere.

See also *BLOGROLL; BULLETIN BOARD SERVICE; ONLINE COMMUNITY; WEBRING*.

blogger
Someone who writes and maintains A BLOG.

blogging
see BLOG.

blogroll
LINKS from one BLOG to other blogs; the process of setting up these links between sites.
Also, creating a blog. Aids for this are known as *blogrolling tools*.

Bluetooth
A short-range WIRELESS NETWORK technology designed to simplify wireless communications, particularly in interfacing with the Internet. It also aims to simplify DATA synchronization between Internet devices and other computers. Bluetooth was originated by several companies, including Ericsson, IBM, Intel, Nokia and Toshiba.

board
see CARD.

boilerplate
A standard piece of text or a graphic, used in memos, reports or letters. The piece is often stored in a SCRAPBOOK and pasted into a DOCUMENT as required. Only minor amendments then need to be made to the document before printing. A boilerplate is similar to a TEMPLATE in nature. Many applications combine them both into the template facility.

bold
A style of text that adds emphasis to a CHARACTER by making it darker and heavier than normal type. The headwords in this book are printed in bold type.

bomb
An unexpected termination of an APPLICATION, similar to a CRASH. This can indicate a serious problem with the HARDWARE, but most often it is caused by a software CONFLICT.

bookmark
Web pages can be bookmarked, or added to the FAVORITES list in the BROWSER, then at a later date, the site can be re-accessed simply by going to Bookmark/Favorites and clicking on the appropriate name.

Boolean search
An INTERNET search using the Boolean operators AND, OR and NOT, from the mathematical logic theory of George Boole. AND, OR and NOT are the primary operations of Boolean logic. In a search, you can specify for each word whether it is to be searched for along with another specified word (AND), searched for as one alternative (OR), or not

boot

searched for at all (NOT). Modern SEARCH ENGINES tend to assume the AND. Advanced search options provide you with the other alternatives.

boot

A ROUTINE designed to make a COMPUTER ready for use. To "boot the system" or INITIALIZE it is to make it ready for normal use. In modern computers, booting the system loads its OPERATING SYSTEM into MEMORY and prepares it to run applications. Within the ROM of a computer is a program that is started when the power is switched on, and this tells the computer to search for the computer's operating system. This is called a *cold boot*. A WARM BOOT is achieved either by pressing the reset button or by pressing the Ctrl/Alt/Del keys simultaneously. On Macintoshes, the best way is via the *Special* menu. This is usually done to unlock a crashed, or frozen, system. Boot is short for bootstrap, by which this process was originally known.

bot

A computer PROGRAM that carries out repetitive tasks, e.g. finding EMAIL addresses, gathering WEB PAGE statistics, providing statistical update from, for instance, the stock market. Short for "robot", and pretty much the same thing as an AGENT. Bots can also be used negatively – *see* BOT WAR; CHAT BOT.

bot war

A situation that arises when two or more interactive chat bots are introduced to a particular CHAT ROOM. The result is usually that the room effectively becomes unusable. *See* BOT; CHAT BOT.

bounced email
An email message that could not be delivered and which is returned to the sender. The cause is very often simply a typing error in the ADDRESS. It may transmit successfully when sent again.

bps (bits per second)
A measure of speed of DATA transmission, especially in connection with the performance of modems. One CHARACTER may require up to 8 or 10 bits to be transmitted, so a MODEM operating at 28 kbps (28,000 bits per second) can transfer two simple pages of text in about one second.

branch
A section of a PROGRAM that causes the program to divert to a SUBROUTINE when certain criteria are met. On completion of the subroutine the program returns to the main activity. The term can also apply to a section of a DIRECTORY.

breadcrumbs
On a WEBSITE, the PATH you have taken to your present location. Breadcrumbs are usually shown as simple text, e.g. *You are here: Home > News > Business > Article* shows that you have arrived at the page "Article" having started at the HOME PAGE and traveled via "News" and "Business". These titles are not necessarily the actual titles of the relevant pages. Each title represents a change of LEVEL in the site hierarchy, and each is also a HYPERLINK to that page. You can, therefore, use breadcrumbs as a kind of "back" BUTTON. *See also* SITE MAP.

broadband

broadband
An ANALOG communications method using high BANDWIDTH. Broadband communications operate at high speeds and can be sent over long distances. The future of the INTERNET is seen to lie in high-speed communications, and, while there are still many obstacles to achieving a true *broadband web*, many users can now access the NET at considerably higher speeds than was previously possible. Such services are offered by both the owners of transmission lines, which could be cable or copper telephone wires, and ISPs. *See also* B-ISDN and ADSL.

broadband integrated services digital network
see B-ISDN.

broken link
The LINK is the means whereby surfing on the INTERNET becomes practicable. On all WEB pages there are links to other parts of the same site, to other sites or to an EMAIL facility. These are often indicated by text that is underlined, is in a different color, or by the MOUSE arrow changing to a pointing hand when a link is crossed. Because of the very fluid nature of the Internet and the frequency with which changes are made, it is often the case that a link becomes inoperable, i.e. broken. When this happens, clicking on a broken link will usually prompt the display of a WEB SERVER ERROR MESSAGE.

browse
To review files or web pages, using, for example, WINDOWS Explorer, or a BROWSER. See also SURFING.

browser
A SOFTWARE program that enables the WEB to be searched, or "surfed". Browsers, such as Microsoft's Internet Explorer and Netscape Navigator, usually include EMAIL, CHAT and other facilities.

bubblejet
see INKJET.

buffer
An electronic memory STORAGE device that is used for temporary storage of DATA passing in or out of the COMPUTER. A common use for a buffer is as a temporary holding area between a slow-moving DEVICE and a fast-moving device, e.g. between a computer and a PRINTER. A buffer therefore allows different parts of the computer system to operate at optimum speeds.

bug
A mistake – a HARDWARE or SOFTWARE error. The term was allegedly first coined in the early days of computing, when a trapped moth was found to have caused a malfunction in a computer. A programming error may be serious and can cause the COMPUTER to perform incorrectly or even CRASH. A very common type of bug is a software CONFLICT.

bulletin board service (BBS)
A computer service set up by organizations or clubs with the aim of providing or exchanging information. It is accessed through a MODEM and can provide entertainment services as well as information.

bundled software

bundled software
SOFTWARE that is provided with a computer as part of the overall purchase price.

burn-in
A period of time during which computer components are tested. CHIPS and other components have a tendency to fail early or late in their lives. Early testing of the computer, say for 48 hours, is recommended before delivery to a customer.

burning; burner
see DISK BURNING; CD BURNING; WRITER.

bus
A channel through which DATA passes. It refers to either the *data bus* (the route data takes to the PROCESSOR) or the *expansion bus* (the route by which data moves to an EXPANSION CARD).

button
An on-screen area in a GRAPHICAL USER INTERFACE computer that is used to select a particular command. Pointing the MOUSE at the button and clicking will select the command.

byte
A combination of eight bits used by the COMPUTER to represent an alphabetical character, a numerical digit or a special character, such as an accent. For example, the letter A is represented by 01000001. A page of text will require slightly more bytes than there are characters to store it, to include spaces, control characters, etc. A

byte

large document will therefore need very many bytes, and computers have millions of bytes (MEGABYTES) of MEMORY. Units that are used most often are the kilobyte and megabyte, representing 1 thousand and 1 million bytes. These are, however, inaccurate because a kilobyte is actually 1,024 bytes and a megabyte 1,048,576 bytes.

C

C or C language
A medium-level computer LANGUAGE developed in 1972 which combines the attributes of both a LOW-LEVEL and a HIGH-LEVEL PROGRAMMING LANGUAGE. Programs in C are easy to read, they can run very quickly, and they can run on most computers.

C++
An object-oriented version of C, widely used in commercial applications. It became popular because it combined C programming with OBJECT-ORIENTED PROGRAMMING. Microsoft's Visual C++ is the most widely used such LANGUAGE.

cable modem
A MODEM that connects the home computer to the NETWORK provided by cable TV companies, to provide a BROADBAND Internet service. It is essentially a network GATEWAY.

cache
An area of RANDOM ACCESS MEMORY in a computer that is used as a temporary STORAGE for frequently used DATA. It allows faster access to the data than if the data were held on a PHYSICAL DRIVE, thus speeding up processing.

CAD (Computer-Aided Design)
special SOFTWARE that will create and manipulate GRAPHICS shapes in the same manner in which an architect or

calculator

designer might operate. The draftsperson can change, edit, save and reprint drawings without the problem of redrawing everything over again. Until quite recently, CAD was kept within the realm of DEDICATED computer systems, but the increased speed, MEMORY and PROCESSING power of modern systems means that it can be undertaken on more ordinary machines. It is used in many disciplines, including architecture, interior design, civil engineering, and mechanical engineering. *See also* AUTOCAD.

CAD/CAM
see CAM.

CAI (Computer-Assisted Instruction)
A form of teaching by COMPUTER. The CAI PROGRAM leads a student through a series of tutorials, question-and-answer sessions, or other tests. The student can use CAI techniques to learn a wide variety of subjects, from computer programming to chess.

calculated field
In a DATABASE MANAGEMENT SYSTEM, a FIELD that contains the result of a FORMULA that may be based on results in other fields. It may also contain dates or logical statements; e.g. a field could be based on the formula:
=if(a<31,Date,'late')
which means that if the value of *a* is less than 31, then put the value in *Date* into the field, otherwise put the word *late* in the field.

calculator
An on-screen UTILITY that can be used in a fashion similar to a hand-held calculator.

CAM (Computer-Aided Manufacture)

CAM (Computer-Aided Manufacture)

The use of computers in manufacturing, which usually refers to the control of robots. The term *CAD/CAM* refers to a system that both designs a product and controls the manufacturing processes. Once a design has been produced by CAD, the design programming controls the production line. This is one of the foundations of flexible manufacturing. See CAD; AUTOCAD.

cancel

If the user has made an error, the COMMAND can be cancelled by pressing the ESCAPE KEY in a DOS OPERATING SYSTEM or by clicking a *cancel button* in a GRAPHICAL USER INTERFACE.

capacity

The amount of information that can be held in a STORAGE device. A 3+-inch FLOPPY DISK typically provides 1.4 megabytes, while a HARD DISK can provide several gigabytes.

capture

To save the information currently displayed. To DIGITIZE an image using, e.g. a SCANNER. To save still or video images in digital form. To record a KEYSTROKE sequence in creating a SHORTCUT KEY (or HOT KEY) or MACRO. *See also* COLOUR REPRODUCTION; SCREEN CAPTURE.

card

A *circuit board* that is made up of plastic backing with circuits etched onto the plastic. Chips are then attached to this base. The card is fitted into a SLOT in the main board of the COMPUTER. Different cards provide different functions such as communications cards, graphic accelerator cards and video capture cards. The main circuit board of a computer is called the MOTHERBOARD.

cartridge
A removable unit used as a secondary, or BACKUP, storage, e.g. magnetic tape or optical disks. In a PRINTER, it is a removable unit that contains the ink or TONER.

cascading style sheets (CSS)
The STYLE SHEET format for HTML documents. Cascading style sheets give developers and users the ability to create style sheets that define how the elements of a document, such as headers and links, will appear. These styles can then be applied to any HTML document. Multiple (cascading) style sheets are applied to the same document.

They enable a designer to define a standard identity for similar, or a family of, documents. There are a number of software TOOLS available for the definition of CSS and many WYSIWYG EDITORS allow for semi-automatic construction.

cascading windows
In a GRAPHICAL USER INTERFACE environment, several windows can be open at any one time. The cascading effect is attained by overlapping the windows so that the title bar of each window is visible.

case sensitive
The ability of a PROGRAM to differentiate between UPPERCASE and lowercase characters. In DOS, it does not matter whether lowercase or uppercase is used, as the operating system is not case sensitive. However, in a case-sensitive search of a DATABASE, a search for "Bill"

Cathode Ray Tube (CRT)

will result in a different found set from a search for "bill". Some WORD PROCESSING programs have the capacity to convert text from lowercase to uppercase characters, and vice versa. Passwords and user names controlling access to online resources are often case sensitive.

Cathode Ray Tube (CRT)

The type of computer VDU that uses an electron gun to fire a beam of electrons at the phosphor screen, much like a television. They are often known as CRT monitors or displays. Standard equipment until fairly recently, they are scheduled to be replaced by the LCD and PLASMA DISPLAY.

CCD (Charged Coupled Device)

see DIGITAL CAMERA.

CD burning

The process of physically recording (or writing) DATA to a CD-ROM, so-called because the burning process is done with a laser in a CD WRITER. Recordable CD-ROMs may be of CD-R or CD-RW format, and have a speed rating (*See* CD-ROM DRIVE; CD-R/CD-RW).

Burning a compact disc normally requires some specialist SOFTWARE, although some operating systems and applications have a basic PLUG-IN (e.g. Windows XP™) with which to do this. Popular packages include Nero and Easy CD Creator for Windows. In Macintosh format, the best-known APPLICATION is called Toast. If a disk is wanted to be equally usable on a PC and a MACINTOSH, it is via Toast that a DUAL-PLATFORM DISK can be created.

There are several standards involved in the CD burning process – ISO9660, JOLIET and UDF, for example. *See also* DVD.

CD-ROM (Compact Disc - Read Only Memory)

CDEV (Control panel DEVice)
A special type of MACINTOSH utility that enables you to adjust basic SYSTEM parameters. Examples are MOUSE settings, KEYBOARD function keys, date and time settings, NETWORK settings, etc. On newer machines, CDEVs are called control panels. *See* CONTROL PANEL.

CD-I (Compact Disc - Interactive)
A standard that refers to the design of systems for viewing audiovisual compact discs using a TV monitor and a CD-I player. Unlike conventional CD-ROM drives, CD-I drives have a built-in MICROPROCESSOR. Although there are some CD-I devices and titles, the format has not become widely accepted.

CD-R/CD-RW
Formats for recordable, blank CD-ROMs. CD-R compact discs can be written to only once. Once the DATA has been burned, it is permanent and cannot be erased. CD-RW compact discs are erasable, and can be rewritten. CD-R discs are compatible with almost all CD players, drives and recorders. CD-RW discs, however, are only compatible with specified devices. Generally, CD-RW is used as a BACKUP disk. It is, however, more expensive and less reliable than CD-R, and so CD-R is often used as a disposable data disk. *See also* CD BURNING; CD-ROM; CD-ROM DRIVE; DISK BURNING; DUAL-PLATFORM DISK.

CD-ROM (Compact Disc - Read Only Memory)
A system invented by Phillips in 1983. CD-ROMs are very useful for holding large amounts of text, graphics, video and audio because they have a storage capacity of

CD-ROM drive

around 700 megabytes, which is equivalent to a quarter of a million pages of plain text. CD-ROMs are commonly used for holding SCANNED IMAGES and are the preferred medium for SOFTWARE programs and for music recordings. DVD continues to threaten to supplant CD-ROM.

See also CD BURNING; CD-R/CD-RW; CD-ROM DRIVE; DISK BURNING; DUAL-PLATFORM DISK.

CD-ROM drive

standard CD-ROM drives are READ-ONLY MEMORY devices. CD-R and CD-RW drives, usually referred to as *writers*, are able to burn CDs as well. CD-ROM drives do not use a magnetic read HEAD, as in a FLOPPY DISK or HARD DISK drive. The head in a CD-ROM drive is a lens that moves from the inside to the outside of the disk. Reflected laser light off the disk surface via this lens allows the DATA on the disk to be reconstituted electronically via a photoelectric cell.

This system avoids many of the problems associated with MAGNETIC MEDIA - there is no direct contact with the disk, so there is no problem with wear and tear (within certain limits) and head crashes are eliminated. Excess vibration, or movement, however, can cause the drive to "skip", or even reset itself. Dirt on the disk can cause problems as well.

CD writers, meanwhile, use the laser to *burn* the data to the disk. In the case of CD-R, this is a physical burn that cannot be altered. CD-RW disks utilize a special film coating that allows for erasing and re-burning of data.

Writers are advertised not only by the formats of disk they can process, but also by their speed, typically given as three numbers, separated by an "x". Each "x"

central processing unit (CPU)

represents 150 kbps data transfer speed. The first number given is the multiplier for CD-R writing, the second that for CD-RW writing, and the third represents the read speed factor. So, a 16x4x24 writer will burn a CD-R at 2,400 kbps, burn a CD-RW at 600 kbps and read a CD-ROM at 3,600 kbps.

CD players/writers can be internally mounted in the computer, or be external devices and are increasingly being produced as combination drives that are also able to play, and burn, DVDs.

See also CD BURNING; CD-ROM; CD-R/CD-RW; DISK BURNING; DUAL-PLATFORM DISK; DVD; PERIPHERAL.

cell
An element or block of a SPREADSHEET into which data, numbers or formulae are placed. A cell is created at the intersection of a column and a row.

censoring the web
The WORLDWIDE WEB is vast and unregulated. It contains much information that is quite unsuitable for children or young people. Programs such as NetNanny, Cybersitter, SurfWatch and Cyber Patrol, and browsers such as Internet Explorer have a special facility to restrict access to inappropriate sites.

central processing unit (CPU)
The core of a COMPUTER system, which contains the INTEGRATED CIRCUITS needed to interpret and execute instructions and perform the basic computer functions. In modern computer systems, it is the integrated circuit that makes use of VLSI (Very Large Scale Integration – up to 100,000 transistors on one

certificate authority

CHIP) to house the control transistors for the computer system.

certificate authority

An organization providing a PUBLIC KEY ENCRYPTION SERVICE, that issues digital certificates, provides public keys and keeps private key information absolutely secure.

CGA (Color Graphics Adapter)

An obsolete VIDEO DISPLAY standard that offered resolutions of 640 x 200 pixels in monochrome and 320 x 200 in four colors. CGA was the first color GRAPHICS system for IBM PCs. It was superseded by VGA.

CGI

Computer-Generated Image. A picture created by computer. *See* COMPUTER ANIMATION.
or
Common Gateway Interface. A specification for transferring information between a WEB SERVER and an APPLICATION, such as a database program. It enables the server to interact with such a program during the process of viewing web pages. A GUEST BOOK is a good example.

CGM (Computer Graphics Metafile)

A file FORMAT for GRAPHICS which uses mainly vector notation.

channel

A set of properties that distinguish individual broadcasts (e.g. TV channels). A CHAT channel covers a specific discussion. *See also* WEBCAST.

character
A single letter, number, space, special character or symbol that can be made to appear on screen by using the KEYBOARD.

character set
The full set of numbers, punctuation marks, alphabetic characters and symbols that a particular COMPUTER SYSTEM uses and that a PRINTER is capable of producing.

characters per inch (cpi)
The number of characters that occupy one inch of text when printed. With a MONOSPACE font, this is an absolute value. For proportionally spaced fonts, it is an average. The larger the type size, the smaller the cpi. Comparison between typefaces and fonts at one type size will show up type density. The greater the cpi, the less space any given text will occupy.

characters per second (cps)
A measurement of the speed at which a PRINTER can produce type, used specifically with reference to an IMPACT PRINTER, e.g. DOT MATRIX and DAISYWHEEL PRINTERS.

chat
REAL TIME communication with other users of the INTERNET, usually done via a CHAT ROOM. Internet Relay Chat was developed in the 1980s. It enables any number of people connected anywhere on the Internet to join in live discussions. To join a chat discussion, you need a CHAT CLIENT and Internet access.

chat bot
A computer PROGRAM that simulates CHAT. Typically, a

chat client

chat bot communicates with a real person, but it is possible for two chat bots to communicate with each other. Chat bots are used in E-COMMERCE customer service, call centers and Internet gaming. Also known as *chatterbots*, or, more properly, *chat robots*.

Bots can be programmed to intrude into chat rooms and carry out acts such as sending large amounts of text to CHAT ROOM participants. When a number of such bots interact with each other, a BOT WAR occurs. *See also* BOT.

chat client

The SOFTWARE needed to be able to participate in a CHAT ROOM. A chat client processes the text entered by a participant and sends it to a CHAT SERVER. Other information is usually also shown, e.g. the identity of the participants who are currently in the room. *See also* CHAT SERVER.

chat room

A VIRTUAL room where chat messages and responses are displayed. Chat rooms are usually accessed via a WEBSITE and are often devoted to particular topics, like a FORUM. But there are many that are open to any subject the participants want to raise. Some are highly sophisticated - participants choose an AVATAR to represent them. Chatting normally requires members to join a CHANNEL first. Participants type their messages into a simple text box and submit it so that all other members can see it and respond in REAL TIME. In this way, there are similarities with TEXT MESSAGING, and experienced "chatters" often use the same type of abbreviations. *See also* CHAT SITE; EMOTICON.

chat server
The SERVER that provides the means of broadcasting messages and responses in a CHAT ROOM. *See also* CHAT CLIENT.

chat site
A WEBSITE that hosts CHAT. All that is required to use such a facility is a BROWSER, but they are often limited in scope and content by the wishes of the site owner.

check box
A small box that is used to TOGGLE between different options in a DIALOG BOX. When the box has a cross or X in it the option is selected; when empty the option is deselected.

check sum
An error detection technique commonly used in data communications. The sending computer performs a calculation on a piece of data, sends the data, and then sends the checksum. The receiving computer takes the sent data, recalculates the checksum, and compares it with the one that was sent. If they match, then no change in the data has occurred; if they do not, the data has been corrupted.

child
see GRANDPARENT; PARENT.

chip
A wafer of silicon that contains minute electronic circuitry and forms the core of a MICROPROCESSOR or computer. After the initial discovery of semiconductors, technological advance was rapid. Early INTEGRATED

chokepoint

CIRCUITS duplicated the functions of a number of electronic components, but now it is possible to create chips that contain unimaginable numbers of components.

In fact, it is possible to have 16 million components on a chip smaller than the tip of a finger. Chips can be mass-produced, and after their design, which is undertaken on an enlarged circuit diagram, the circuitry is transferred to plates called photomasks. Using a succession of photomasks, the chip is coated with materials that result in several layers of doped SILICON, and it then forms the equivalent of a highly complex electronic circuit.

chokepoint

A point in a NETWORK through which a large amount of TRAFFIC flows. As this exposes a vulnerability, one of the main aims of a network designer is to eliminate chokepoints.

chooser

A UTILITY for the APPLE MACINTOSH that controls the selection of printers, fax cards and file servers. Once a device is selected, every application can use the device without the necessity for further selections to be set up.

circuit board

see CARD.

circular reference

A situation occurring in a SPREADSHEET that is the result of a CELL containing a FORMULA that depends on the result of the formula. For example, cell *a7* could contain the formula "sum (a1.a5)" in which the cell *a1* contains the formula "=a7". The calculation cannot therefore be completed until *a7* has a total, and this total will change each time a summation occurs. This process could go on forever in a circular fashion. The user can stop the process by limiting the number of ITERATIONS that can occur.

CISC (Complex Instruction Set Computer)

A type of processor CHIP in which an instruction may take several operations and cycles to execute. (*See also* RISC.)

clear

A COMMAND that is used to remove a part of a DOCUMENT. This may be an unwanted paragraph or sentence from a document in a word processing PROGRAM or a selection of cells from a SPREADSHEET. Clear commands can usually not be undone until another command is selected. It is important to ensure that you really wanted to clear the selection before you move on to the next command.

click

To press and release the MOUSE button. This procedure is done with the left-hand button in order to select an item such as an option in a CHECK BOX. The mouse pointer is positioned over the check box, the mouse button is clicked and the check box is selected. *See also* DOUBLE CLICK; RIGHT CLICK; DRAG AND DROP.

client

A personal computer or WORKSTATION in a LOCAL AREA NETWORK that is used to request information from a network's FILE SERVER.

client document

client document
A DOCUMENT that is connected to another document (primary) in another computer on a NETWORK. When the primary document is updated the client document is also updated immediately.

client/server
A type of networking where the user's computer has few RESOURCES, is only used for running applications, and relies on the network servers to manage operations like printing, network traffic, files, etc.
Also applications that run in this ENVIRONMENT and which only provide a user with a certain amount of USER INTERFACE. *See also* FRONT OFFICE; BACK OFFICE; PEER-TO-PEER.

clip art
A collection of ready-drawn pieces of art that are available to copy and paste into any document. The purpose is to enhance the look of the document, whether it is a newsletter or promotional flyer. Many GRAPHICS packages provide thousands of pieces of clip art.

clipboard
A temporary STORAGE area for any selection of a DOCUMENT resulting from a CUT AND PASTE or COPY AND PASTE command. The clipboard holds the text or graphics after the copy command is issued and until the paste command is issued, at which point the text or graphic is placed into the active document at the selected place.

clipping path
In editing an image in a GRAPHICS application, a drawn

CMYK (Cyan, Magenta, Yellow, Key)

or plotted outline of an image area that serves as a MASK. Only the part within the clipping path is saved, allowing it to be placed in another application or document. *See also* DRAW PROGRAM; MASK; PAINT PROGRAM; PLOT.

clock speed
A description of the speed of a MICROPROCESSOR, usually described in megahertz (one million cycles per second). The system clock emits a stream of electrical pulses or clicks that synchronize all the processor's activities.

clone
The original name given to computers that succeeded in replicating the features of an IBM personal computer. Many companies now produce computers that are compatible with the IBM PC but have more features, better components and are built to higher specifications.

close
The command to finish working with a computer file. In a GRAPHICAL USER INTERFACE environment, several windows can be open at any one time. Each window has a *close box* that, when checked (*see* CHECK BOX), closes the WINDOW.

CMOS (Complementary Metal-Oxide Semiconductor)
A chip that features low power consumption.

CMYK (Cyan, Magenta, Yellow, Key)
A color model for printed images, in which all colors can be represented by a mixture of the three *subtractive primary colors*, plus black (the key). In order to produce

coaxial cable

this mixture, four *color separations* are required, which, when used with the appropriate ink, will print on the same piece of paper a reproduction of the image. This is the basis of *four-color (process) printing*. These colors are often described as PROCESS COLORS. In computer parlance, this process is known as DITHERING. *See also* COLOR REPRODUCTION; COLOR SEPARATION; RGB; SCREEN.

coaxial cable
A cable of the type used for connecting television aerials. It is constructed of an insulated central wire with surrounding copper mesh enclosed in a plastic cover. This cable type is used in network systems such as ETHERNET as it can carry quite a lot of data and is shielded against interference.

COBOL (COmmon Business Oriented Language)
One of the most commonly-used computer programming languages for large MAINFRAME business applications. It has never achieved the popularity of BASIC on smaller computers such as PCs. For large businesses, however, it became the choice for invoicing, salary records and stock control because its programs are easy to read and amend. Its function is to store, retrieve and process such DATA, and it therefore became useful in automating such processes.

code
A list of instructions written to solve a particular problem. It is also another way of saying "to program". The term is a bit vague. The code that a programmer writes is called SOURCE CODE. After it has been compiled, it is called OBJECT CODE. Code that is ready to run is called MACHINE CODE.

color reproduction

codec (COmpressor/DECompressor)
Software that compresses and decompresses audio and video samples in order to speed up transmission and save on STORAGE. Codecs may also be able to translate from one FORMAT to another. Also software that provides general FILE COMPRESSION.

cold boot
see BOOT

color monitor
A VDU that displays images in multicolor.

color separation
To reproduce a color image in print, it is necessary to separate the image into several component color versions. The image can be scanned or photographed using filters to produce four separate versions representing the "value" in the image of each *reflective primary color* – blue (cyan), red (magenta) and yellow, plus black.

In commercial printing, these separations are used to produce printing plates for each color, used together on one machine in *four-color process printing*. *See* COLOR REPRODUCTION; CMYK; DITHERING; RGB; SCANNER; SCREEN; RESOLUTION.

color reproduction
Everything we see can be represented by a combination of primary colors (that is, colors that cannot be produced by mixing other colors).

In print, the image is seen via reflected light. In this case, the primary colors are cyan (a shade of blue),

color reproduction

magenta (a shade of red), and yellow. These are known as the *subtractive* or *reflective* primaries. Mixing equal amounts of each produces black (actually a shade of brown).

A color image is therefore reproduced in print by breaking the image down into its component primary colors (*see* COLOR SEPARATION). Because the mixed black is quite weak, a fourth filtered image is produced to represent pure black – this is known as "key". Hence, reproduction using this four-color process is referred to as CMYK.

When the separations are made, they are also filtered through a SCREEN, which breaks the image into dots – the denser the image area, the denser the dots. The screen can be physical or VIRTUAL and the "fineness" of the screen determines the RESOLUTION of the image.

In four-color print, the screen for each primary has a different mesh angle; the result being that the dots for each separation are slightly out of alignment – this ensures that they do not print over each other. When the image from each separation is printed onto the same piece of paper, the original image seems to be reproduced (although it's actually an optical illusion). In computer parlance, this process is known as DITHERING.

On video displays, the image is seen via transmitted light. Here, the primary colors are red, green and blue. These are known as the *additive*, or *transmissive* primaries. Mixing equal amounts of each produces white. Image reproduction on video displays is known as RGB.

When an image is *scanned* or otherwise turned into a computer file, it is *digitized*, which breaks the image into a collection of dots, much as if it had been *screened* for print. The greater the dpi, the greater the image resolution.

All color computer monitors are RGB monitors, consisting, in the case of a CRT, of a vacuum tube with three electron guns – one each for red, green, and blue – that fire electrons at the phosphor-coated screen. When the phosphors are excited by the electron beams, they glow. The three beams converge (approximately) for each point on the screen so that each PIXEL is a combination of the three colors. A pixel is made up of bits, so that any image that has been digitized (e.g. scanned) can be represented by RGB. *See also* bitmap; LCD; PLASMA DISPLAY.

column
In a SPREADSHEET program a column is a vertical block of CELLS that extends from the top to the bottom of the spreadsheet. The column is usually identified by an alphanumeric character. In a word processing program a column is normally a newspaper style column in which the text flows from the bottom of one column to the top of the next column on the same or succeeding page.

COMDEX
The largest computer show in the world. It takes place in the USA in November every year and is for the trade, rather than the consumer. There are now COMDEX exhibitions held regularly around the world.

comma delimited file
A method of saving a file in which each data FIELD is separated by a comma. The comma is a DELIMITER that

command

indicates the end of one field of DATA and the beginning of the next (or the end of the FILE). Other common types of delimiter are the TAB and the paragraph TAG. Saving a file in this way makes it easier to transfer files between different programs or computers. *See also* RICH TEXT FORMAT.

command

An instruction or set of instructions that will start or stop an operation in a computer PROGRAM, e.g. *run, print, exit*.

command button

A BUTTON appearing in a DIALOG BOX that initiates a COMMAND such as *continue with the operation, cancel the operation* or *help*.

command key

On a MACINTOSH keyboard, a special KEY that is used in conjunction with other keys to provide shortcuts for commands. All Macintosh programs use the same command shortcuts.

command line

A line of instructions or commands INPUT to the computer through a KEYBOARD. For example, *format a:* could be typed to tell the computer to FORMAT a disk on the *a:* drive.

command.com

An essential command FILE that is required for DOS to run. The file controls the on-screen prompts, interprets the typed commands and executes the required operations. *See also* CONFIG.SYS; AUTOEXEC.BAT

communications settings

common gateway interface
see CGI.

communications port
A PORT at the rear of a COMPUTER into which a serial device such as a PRINTER or a MODEM can be plugged. *See also* PARALLEL PORT; SERIAL COMMUNICATION; EPP

communications program
A PROGRAM that allows a COMPUTER to connect with another computer. This can be achieved via direct or remote connection to a NETWORK, or by a specific cable connection. Communications programs include telephone directories, facilities that automate the dial-up process, log-on procedures, and network configuration software. *See also* WIZARD.

communications protocol
A list of standards that control the transfer of information or exchange of DATA between computers connected to a NETWORK. The PROTOCOL will include such definitions as rate of transmission, whether it will be SYNCHRONOUS or not, coding and decoding and error recovery. Generally speaking, such protocols are built into the relevant HARDWARE. Some better-known examples are Kermit and Xmodem. See also ASYNCHRONOUS COMMUNICATION; COMMUNICATIONS SETTINGS.

communications settings
When you access an ONLINE SERVICE you must set your computer to the same set of standards as the SERVER. The main standards are BAUD RATE, PARITY BIT, DATA BITS, STOP BITS, DUPLEX, and HANDSHAKING.

community

community
The population of an ONLINE INFORMATION SERVICE or BULLETIN BOARD SERVICE, which expresses itself in conferences, discussion boards, forums and chat rooms

Compact Disc
see CD ROM.

Compact Disc - Interactive
see CDI.

Compaq
A major manufacturer of high-quality IBM-compatible computers, now a part of Hewlett-Packard.

compatible
A characteristic that permits one machine to accept and process DATA prepared by another machine, without conversion. It can also refer to hardware such as printers and monitors.

To be really compatible, it should be possible for a PROGRAM or PERIPHERAL to run on a SYSTEM with no modification and with everything running as intended. *See also* BACKWARD COMPATIBLE.

compiler
A PROGRAM that translates CODE that has been written in a HIGH-LEVEL PROGRAMMING LANGUAGE into an EXECUTABLE PROGRAM. *See also* OBJECT CODE.

compress
To reduce the space (amount of RAM) taken up by files in order to optimize MEMORY use and increase the amount

of DATA that can be stored, and the ease (speed) with which it can be transmitted to another computer (*See also* FILE COMPRESSION.)

CompuServe
An ONLINE INFORMATION SERVICE provider that provides a wide variety of services such as EMAIL, news services, sports results and information, encyclopedia, financial information, computer information, many online forums and files to download and INTERNET ACCESS. CompuServe was the pioneer company in this field, but is now part of AOL.

computer
An electronic DATA PROCESSING device, capable of accepting data, applying a prescribed set of instructions to the data, and displaying the result in some manner or form. Also any CONFIGURATION of the devices that are interconnected and programmed to operate as a computer SYSTEM. Typically, this includes a CENTRAL PROCESSING UNIT with KEYBOARD, DISPLAY, PRINTER and some form of DISK DRIVE.

computer animation
The process of providing some form of moving image from a series of still images. There are many SOFTWARE applications that enable you to create animations, ranging from simple image file animation to much more complex MULTIMEDIA packages, providing the whole range of sound and vision facilities.

computer literacy
To have some expertise and familiarity with computers.

computer system

The term generally refers to the use of applications, the ability to set up and maintain a system, and at least a basic understanding of how it all works.

computer system
see SYSTEM.

computer-aided design
see CAD.

computer-generated image
see CGI.

concatenation
The adding of two or more fields, or pieces of text, together to form one item, commonly used in SPREADSHEET or DATABASE MANAGEMENT SYSTEMS to manipulate data.

concordance file
A file that contains a list of words that are to appear in an INDEX. The WORD PROCESSING program uses the concordance file to create the index along with the page numbers that relate to the index words.

condensed type
A TYPE STYLE that reduces the width of characters, or the space between them, so that more characters are printed per inch of space. *See also* EXPANDED TYPE; KERN.

conditional statement
A statement used in computer PROGRAMMING to determine the next operation. Conditional statements

are also used in SPREADSHEET and DATABASE programming. For example, a salesman's commission can be calculated with a conditional statement such as:
=if(sales>=5000, sales*.10, 400)
which means that if the salesman generates sales greater than $5,000, then a 10 per cent commission is payable, otherwise a flat rate commission of $400 is due. In other words, the result is *conditional* on the level of sales.

config.sys

A DOS file that contains commands that set up the computer's OPERATING SYSTEM. DOS requires that peripherals and applications have specific start commands that are held in the config.sys file. It is therefore important that the file is not deleted or the various programs or peripherals will not function properly.

configuration

The machines that are interconnected and programmed to operate as a COMPUTER SYSTEM. Typically, this includes a CENTRAL PROCESSING UNIT with KEYBOARD, DISPLAY, PRINTER and some form of DISK DRIVE. It also refers to the setting up of a computer system or PROGRAM to ensure that it matches the needs of the user. Configuration has to be performed at the outset, and while modern applications SOFTWARE has automated the procedure to some extent, there are certain elements that have to be done manually. Once established, the SET-UP is saved in a configuration file that should not be erased or altered.

conflict

A mismatch between two or more elements of a SYSTEM,

connect time

which leads to error messages and system instability. Much less common than it used to be, largely due to the advent of PLUG AND PLAY. Conflicts could originate with SOFTWARE or HARDWARE. A *version conflict* can occur when a newer version of a FILE is already on your HARD DISK when you are carrying out an APPLICATION installation. A DRIVER conflict occurs when one or more DEVICE drivers interfere with each other, or even with the OPERATING SYSTEM, leading to a CRASH. *See also* IRQ.

connect time

one basis of charging customers for using an ONLINE SERVICE. The charge relates directly to the amount of time spent connected to the system. As the INTERNET has developed, subscription (or even prepayment) systems have been adopted instead. Now, Internet access for no charge is the norm, although one does have to pay for the method of connection, whether to the telephone company or the ISP, or both.

console

Another term for a TERMINAL, at the very least comprising a MONITOR and KEYBOARD. It usually refers to a terminal attached to a NETWORK SERVER or MAINFRAME, used to monitor the system status.

The term is also commonly used to describe the GUI in a particular APPLICATION, particularly one that requires a large measure of control, where there may be a virtual EMULATION of a physical control panel, e.g. in a MEDIA PLAYER.

constant

A fixed value used in a SPREADSHEET. When using a

continuous tone

spreadsheet program, the use of constants has to be carefully monitored. Where possible, constants in repeated formulae should be avoided. One constant in a primary CELL should be used, and all the repeat formulae should be based on the primary cell. If the constant in the primary cell is changed, all repeat formulae will automatically change.

content provider
A company that provides material for publication on another company's WEBSITE or online service. This may cover topics such as news, weather, sport, reviews and so on.

context sensitive help
An information system incorporated into an APPLICATION that automatically finds the relevant information to assist with a COMMAND or operation with which the user is having difficulty. Context sensitive help systems reduce the time that is spent searching through HELP files for the appropriate section, thus making the program more user-friendly and allowing the user to be more productive.

continuous tone
images that have a continuous range of color or gray hues, shades and tones, e.g. photographs or TV images. To reproduce such an image in print or on a computer, it has to be converted into another form by filtering it through a SCREEN, scanning it, or otherwise digitizing it, which converts the image into a collection of dots – the density of the dots corresponding to the density of the image area. Converting a black-and-white

continuous-tone printer

continuous tone image into a DIGITAL image is known as *gray scaling*. The end product is known as a HALFTONE. *See also* COLOR REPRODUCTION; GRAY SCALE.

continuous-tone printer

A color printer that prints dots with varying amounts of cyan, magenta, and yellow on top of one another to form a dot of the appropriate color. As this does not require multiple dots to give the impression of a single color, it tends to produce equivalent output at lower resolutions, e.g. 300 dpi. To compete, printers that utilize DITHERING have to provide resolutions of 600 (or even 1200) by 600 dpi. *See also* COLOR REPRODUCTION; CONTINUOUS TONE; CMYK.

control panel

A UTILITY designed to allow the user to alter the look and feel of the computer environment. These utilities control such aspects as screen colors, monitor settings, date and time display, sound and speech settings, mouse controls, etc. (*See also* CDEV.)

control panel device

see CDEV.

cookie

A small FILE created by a WEB SERVER which is transmitted to, and stored on, the HARD DISK of the computer making the connection. It is used to store information about the session to assist in future sessions, e.g. helping to recognize the user and prepare information personal to them, or to provide recommendations, personalized web pages, etc. The cookie is then read by the server next time the user visits the site.

copy and paste

Cookies are necessary for E-COMMERCE, particularly, because HTTP is a stateless PROTOCOL – it has no knowledge of previous activity. Cookies are sometimes regarded with suspicion by users – what information do they hold? They can also be vulnerable to attack by SPYWARE, and can in themselves be pernicious. For this reason, regular cleaning out of cookies is highly recommended, even though you may then have to start over with a favorite WEBSITE. For this reason also, browsers such as INTERNET EXPLORER have adjustable settings that control how cookies are handled. It is worth noting that some websites will not be accessible without allowing cookies onto your computer.

coprocessor
A secondary or support CHIP that is used alongside the main chip to provide added power for specific operations, such as graphics display or mathematical calculations.

copy
To create a duplicate of a FILE, graphic, program or disk without changing the original version. Some copy-protected programs, however, do not allow an exact copy of an original to be made. With a GUI, copying is generally done via DRAG AND DROP.

copy and paste
To COPY a piece of DATA to the CLIPBOARD or other BUFFER, using a GUI, and then duplicating it somewhere else. This could be done with text in a word processor document, a file, a directory, or even the whole content of a disk. In WINDOWS, the main buffer for this operation is the TEMP FILE. *See also* CUT AND PASTE.

copy protection

copy protection
A method of preventing, or at least reducing, the user's ability to copy a program illegally. A special CODE is written into the PROGRAM that requires the user to type in a PASSWORD or insert a special disk in order to use the program.

corrupted file
A FILE or part of a file that has become unreadable. Causes of file corruption include improper handling of a disk, a power surge, VIRUS activity, flaws on the disk surface or damaged READ/WRITE HEADS.

country code
see DOMAIN NAME.

CP/M (Control Program Monitor)
The operating system that dominated the desktop computer world before DOS was introduced in 1981. Control Program Monitor was the trade name used for the operating system for microcomputers based on the Z80 microprocessor chip.

cpi
see CHARACTERS PER INCH.

cps
see CHARACTERS PER SECOND.

CPU
see CENTRAL PROCESSING UNIT.

crack
To break the COPY PROTECTION and registration aspects

cryptography

of an APPLICATION, thus allowing an illegal copy to be made, or a DEMO version to be converted into the full version without paying for it. These are forms of PIRACY.

To break into a system. Crackers are taken to be people whose single aim is to break through the security systems surrounding a site, network or application, whereas a HACKER is someone who finds and exploits weaknesses in programs and systems, often for what, to them, is a practical joke.

crash
An unexpected termination of an APPLICATION, usually resulting in the freezing of the computer, i.e. it becomes completely unresponsive. The computer often has to be *rebooted* to recover. These days, most applications have the ability to easily recover data that was in use at the time of the crash. (*see* BOOT).

cropping
A feature of GRAPHICS programs that allows electronic trimming of a picture either to get rid of unwanted parts of the image or to fit the image into a predefined space.

cross-platform
Applies to the use of SOFTWARE and files on computers with a different OPERATING SYSTEM and/or hardware platform, e.g. MACINTOSH and PC/WINDOWS. *See also* DUAL-PLATFORM DISK.

CRT
see CATHODE RAY TUBE.

cryptography
The process of converting DATA into a secret code that

CSS

allows the data to be transmitted safely over a NETWORK without violation. The conversion is achieved by using what is called an ENCRYPTION algorithm which changes plain text (the original) into cipher text (the equivalent of the original in coded form). At the receiving end, the cipher text is converted back to plain text, a process called decoding or DECRYPTION.

CSS

see CASCADING STYLE SHEETS.

cursor

An indicator on the screen of a VDU, used by a COMPUTER to direct a user to the starting position – the point at which DATA can be entered. It can be a small line, a square of light on the screen or an arrow symbol, and can be controlled by use of the MOUSE or the arrow keys on the numeric pad on the right-hand side of the KEYBOARD.

custom software

A computer PROGRAM that is written specifically to match the systems that the client operates in his or her business. The program is useful only to one client and will probably not be usable by others.

cut and paste

In a GUI, to select a piece of text, an image, a file or directory, move it to the CLIPBOARD or other BUFFER, and then move it to the desired end location. *See also* COPY AND PASTE.

cyber café

A café where customers can browse the INTERNET, play

computer games or look at CDs, as well as consume drinks and snacks. Customers are generally charged per minute for Internet access. Also known as an INTERNET CAFE. Very useful for students, travelers and the low-waged.

cyber luddite
Someone who is against the WORLDWIDE WEB on principle, usually involving some aspect of anti-globalization.

cyberchondriac
Someone who is obsessed with the conviction that their COMPUTER continuously malfunctions. This is usually because they have not read the instructions or manual. The sort of person who always blames their tools.

cybercrud
Although this can refer to computer jargonese, it usually stands for unwanted text in an EMAIL message, such as that showing the route the message took to get to the recipient's computer.

cyberia
A withdrawn state of mind often achieved by programmers when developing or debugging SOFTWARE, brought about by total concentration. Also the physical isolation which is a result of this.

cybermediary
An intermediary between a customer and one or more companies, e.g. a WEB insurance broker or travel agent. Many of the most successful e-businesses work like this, almost acting as mini-search engines for a specific

cybernaut

subject area. Outside of computing, they would be known as "middle men".

cybernaut
Originally, someone who utilized special equipment and devices to enjoy VIRTUAL REALITY. Now it refers more to anyone who enthusiastically explores the INTERNET.

cybernetics
A branch of science that is concerned with COMPUTER control systems and the relationship between these artificial systems and biological systems.

cyberphobia
Genuine fear of computers, INFORMATION TECHNOLOGY and the INTERNET, usually boiling down to a general fear of the new and of inadequacy, seeing the world of computing as being intimidating.

cyberpunk
Originally a genre of science fiction literature, characterized by a dystopic vision of an oppressive society dominated by computer technology, but also possessing an anarchic subculture that owed much to 1980s punk. It was originated by William Gibson in his novel *Neuromancer*.

Increasingly, it refers more to a beatnik-type movement within "digital culture", encompassing contemporary counterculture – a new underground.

cybersitter
Computer-literate youngsters who earn some extra cash by teaching other children some COMPUTER and INTERNET skills.

cyberspace
In modern computer communications, a user connects with cyberspace when he or she logs on to an online service or connects with another computer. Electronic mail and forum messages move around cyberspace. The word was thought up by William Gibson, in his novel *Neuromancer*.

cyberspeak
The gamut of computer jargon, almost forming another language, used enthusiastically by those in the know and generally intimidating to those who are not. A prime source of CYBERPHOBIA.

cybersquatting
Buying a DOMAIN NAME that features the name of a celebrity or a well-known company. There are a number of motives for this, and few of them are very positive.. The buyer might want to embarrass the celebrity or compromise the company. There are also commercial reasons - a domain name featuring that of an up and coming company could be sold for a profit, although this is a lot like hostage-taking. Sites featuring famous names, however, attract visitors and this makes them of interest to advertisers – a valid enough reason for a WEBSITE creator. There have recently been some successful prosecutions in this area.

cyberstalker
Someone who stalks an individual by means of the INTERNET, usually via EMAIL, SEARCH ENGINES and by abusing subscriptions to directory providers.

D

daisywheel printer
An old-fashioned printer that worked by rotating a print element resembling a wheel with spokes. Each spoke contained two characters of the alphabet. Daisywheel printers have been overtaken by INKJET and LASER PRINTERS.

data
Information; a group of facts, concepts, symbols, numbers, letters, or instructions that can be used to communicate, make decisions, etc.

data bits
During ASYNCHRONOUS COMMUNICATION, the elements of a sent CHARACTER that contain the actual DATA. *See also* CHECKSUM; PARITY BIT.

data bus
see BUS.

data file
A computer FILE containing DATA, as opposed to an APPLICATION or PROGRAM.

data processing
The preparing and storing, handling or processing of DATA through a COMPUTER.

database
A file of information (DATA) that is stored on a COMPUTER

in a structured manner and used by a computer PROGRAM such as a DATABASE MANAGEMENT SYSTEM. Information is usually subdivided into particular data FIELDS, i.e. a space for a specific item of information.

database management system (DBMS)
A SOFTWARE system for managing the storage, access, updating and maintenance of a DATABASE. Users can edit the database, save the data, and extract reports from the database. There are many software packages that enable the creation and manipulation of data in databases. More commonly, the DBMS and the database files are combined into one package, known generically as a database.

daughter board
A *printed circuit board* that plugs into the main board, or MOTHERBOARD, in a computer with the purpose of adding processing power or other facilities. *See also* CARD.

DBMS
see DATABASE MANAGEMENT SYSTEM.

DDR (Double Data Rate)
An SDRAM memory CHIP that can increase performance by doubling the effective data rate of the BUS.

debug
To locate and correct errors occurring in a APPLICATION, e.g. when writing the CODE for a PROGRAM there will undoubtedly be mistakes made. In order to make the program work correctly the errors must be eliminated. The program must be "debugged." *See also* BUG.

decollator

decollator
A machine that separates the sheets of a multipart form or continuous paper, i.e. it separates the top sheet from the second sheet.

decryption
The process of decoding or deciphering DATA from an encrypted form (*see* ENCRYPTION) in order that the data can be read and used.

dedicated
A term that describes a COMPUTER or hardware DEVICE that is used solely for one purpose, e.g. when a computer is dedicated to act as a SERVER for a NETWORK.

dedicated line
A communications link that is dedicated exclusively to a particular function. For example, a dedicated line may be used in a building to connect up a number of computers, or a security system.

default
A pre-set PREFERENCE out of a series of options in a PROGRAM. For example, in a WORD PROCESSOR the defaults for style of type and font may have the value of SANS SERIF 12 BOLD. These settings can be reset and will do so automatically under certain circumstances.

defragment
To clean up the HARD DISK by rearranging files into contiguous order. Because the OPERATING SYSTEM stores new data in whatever free space is available, data files become spread out across the disk. Defragging puts

demo (short for demonstration)

everything together in a neat and tidy way and used to be a maintenance necessity. Performance increases may not be very noticeable on modern computers running routine APPLICATIONS, however. Nevertheless, it is still good practice because it reduces wear and tear on the drive mechanism.

degauss
To remove the effects of a magnetic field, used of CRT monitors and DEVICES. These devices create magnetic fields in the course of their operation, and these fields can cause display distortion. Consequently, most MONITORS automatically degauss the CRT whenever you turn them on. In addition, they usually have a manual degaussing facility via the monitor menu.

delete
To erase a character, word, command or program. Once the item is deleted, it may not be possible to RECOVER it, so it is important to be careful about which files, etc, are deleted. GUI operating systems usually make use of a UTILITY called a waste bin, or something similar, which allows you to mark files for deletion, but not to do so unless you really want to.

delimiter
A CHARACTER that is used to show the end of a COMMAND or the end of a FIELD of data in a data record. Characters commonly used as delimiters are the comma (,), semi-colon (;) or tab. *See also* COMMA DELIMITED FILE.

demo (*short for* demonstration)
A PROGRAM that is restricted in some way but still shows

demodulation

a potential user the main features of the program. Inevitably, *demo disks* are used to promote and sell SOFTWARE, although demo versions are more frequently available for direct DOWNLOAD from a WEBSITE, requiring the purchase of a LICENCE KEY to unlock the program and use all of its features. *See also* CRACK.

demodulation
see MODEM.

density
A measure of the amount of information (in BITS) that can be stored on magnetic media, such as a FLOPPY DISK, which can be single density, double density, or high density, using very fine-grained magnetic particles. A double density 3.5 inch disk could hold 740Kb of data – a high density 3.5 inch disk, 1.44Mb.

descending order
see ASCENDING ORDER.

desk accessory
A small UTILITY program that can help in a computer user's productivity. Desk accessories include items such as notebooks, address books, on-screen calculators and scrapbooks.

desktop
In an OPERATING SYSTEM environment that uses a GRAPHICAL USER INTERFACE, the desktop is the computer representation of a physical desk top on to which files and folders can be placed.

Desktop publishing (DTP)
The software and hardware that makes possible the composition of text and graphics and the production of complex documents at your own desk. With a COMPUTER, PRINTER, and various programs to prepare and print documents, it is possible to produce anything from a single page of text to advertisements, pamphlets, books and magazines.

Computer-aided publishing has been possible since the early 1970s. Desktop publishing as a function of PERSONAL COMPUTERS became possible with the introduction in 1985 of the first relatively inexpensive LASER PRINTER producing LETTER QUALITY for type and visuals.

developer
Someone who designs and writes SOFTWARE. Generally, it refers to people working in the commercial software field, but it can also refer to a professional within an organization in another field.

device
Any machine or component that attaches to a COMPUTER. Examples include disk drives, printers, mice, and modems. *External devices* like these are better known as *peripherals*.

Most devices require a program called a DEVICE DRIVER, that converts general commands from an APPLICATION into specific commands that the device understands. *See also* PERIPHERAL.

device driver
A UTILITY that extends the capabilities of the OPERATING

DHTML

SYSTEM to allow HARDWARE devices such as a MOUSE, CD ROM DRIVE, PRINTER or HARD DISK to work with the computer.

DHTML
see DYNAMIC HTML.

diagnostic
A UTILITY designed to test computer hardware and operating systems for errors that may cause or be causing an ERROR MESSAGE.

dialog box
A WINDOW that is an integral part of a PROGRAM and is used to convey information or request information from the user about the operations of the program. A dialog box can have: OPTION buttons, which are "either/or" buttons; CHECK BOXES, which allow several options from a menu to be selected; LIST BOXES, which present a list of options, one of which can be selected; and COMMAND BUTTONS, which allow the user to continue the operation with the selection, or to cancel the operation.

dial-up access
Connecting to a NETWORK via a MODEM and a telephone line. The line is often also used for phone calls. This form of access is the opposite of a DEDICATED LINE.

dial-up account
The basic account provided by an INTERNET SERVICE PROVIDER. Access to the Internet is via the telephone line and using a MODEM.

dial-up networking (DUN)
Working on a NETWORK via DIAL-UP ACCESS The Internet was originally an example of a network which was based on this form of networking. Also a component of WINDOWS that enables such networking.

DUN is the original method of REMOTE ACCESS.

digispeak
In online communications, the use of acronyms to replace common phrases, e.g. BTW for "by the way" and IMHO for "in my humble opinion." These shortcuts are turning into a new language. *See also* ACRONYM; CYBERSPEAK; NETIQUETTE; TEXT MESSAGING.

digital
A term used to describe the use of two states, on or off, in order to represent all DATA. A COMPUTER is digital since it represents all data in a series of 1s and 0s. These two states equate to the switching on and off of current in electric circuits, which is the basis of a PROCESSOR.

The opposite of digital is ANALOG. Humans experience the world analogically. Vision, for example, is an analog experience, with CONTINUOUS TONE, but, like most analog events, it can be simulated digitally, e.g. a HALFTONE. Digital representations of analog events are therefore approximations, albeit ones that can work well.

digital camera
A camera that records and stores images digitally. As with all DIGITAL devices, there is a maximum RESOLUTION and number of colors that can be represented. Digital cameras record images as RGB, which are stored as variable charges on a *charged coupled device* (CCD) or

digital certificate

CMOS chip. The *analog-to-digital converter* (ADC) then converts the charge to digital data and passes it to the *digital signal processor* (DSP), which recreates the image, allows you to view it, and store it in the camera's FLASH MEMORY. Images can then be downloaded to computer or printer by USB cable, or MEMORY CARD reader.

Digital photographs can be viewed instantly, they can be deleted instantly, they can be edited by IMAGE EDITORS, and they can be taken at a choice of resolutions. They are, however, limited by the amount of memory in the camera, the optical resolution of the digitizing mechanism, and, finally, by the resolution of the final output device.

Digital video cameras use the same IMAGING methods, as well as SAMPLING, to produce a moving image. *See* COLOR REPRODUCTION.

digital certificate

An encrypted ATTACHMENT to an electronic message for security purposes, most commonly to verify that a message sender is whom they claim to be, and also to provide the receiver with the means to encrypt a reply. An individual wishing to send an encrypted message applies for a certificate from a CERTIFICATE AUTHORITY. The authority issues an encrypted digital certificate containing the sender's PUBLIC KEY, and the sender encrypts the message using the recipient's public key.

The recipient of the encrypted message uses their PRIVATE KEY to decode the certificate, and so obtains the sender's public key and identification information held within the certificate. With this information, the recipient can send an encrypted reply.

digital signature

Only the public key can be used to encrypt messages and only the corresponding private key can be used to decrypt them. It is impossible to deduce the private key if you know the public key.

For digital certificates to be successful, the certificate authority has to be able to guarantee that the private keys are securely stored, and, of course, one has to know the recipient's public key in advance. *See also* SECURED ELECTRONIC TRANSACTION STANDARD; DECRYPTION; ENCRYPTION; PUBLIC KEY ENCRYPTION SYSTEM.

digital money

money in electronic form to make purchases via the INTERNET. To operate financial transactions securely, software has been developed to ensure complete safety. There are several security protocols and on many browsers, a secure connection is signified by a key or padlock icon on the screen being closed rather than open. This enables credit card transactions to be undertaken. *See* PAYMENT PROTOCOL; SMART CARD; SSL.

Digital Research

A major manufacturer of computers, including IBM-compatible machines. It was formed in 1957. It also created its own operating system, DR-DOS, similar to MS-DOS, which was, for a while, an open competitor to Microsoft's product..

digital signature

An electronic version of a signature which is encrypted and sent with a message. This guarantees that the recipient gets a document that has not been read by an unauthorized person. To prove the validity of the

digital subscriber line

message and the sender, a DIGITAL CERTIFICATE is required. In effect this is an identification issued by specific certification organizations and contains the following information: name, address, company; PUBLIC KEY (the published part of a two-part cryptographic system); serial number and ID; and the digital signature. *See also* CERTIFICATION AUTHORITY; PUBLIC KEY ENCRYPTION SERVICE.

digital subscriber line
see DSL.

digital video camera
see DIGITAL CAMERA.

Digital Video/Versatile Disc (DVD)
An OPTICAL DISK technology similar to CD-ROM. A DVD holds a minimum of 4.7Gb of DATA, can be recorded on both sides and has more than one layer. DVDs are the new standard medium for digital representation of movies and other multimedia presentations.

There are various specifications for DVDs, covering DVD-video, DVD-audio and data-DVD. One of the best features of DVD drives is that they are BACKWARD COMPATIBLE with CD-ROMs.

DVD-video uses MPEG video compression, which provides about two hours play time per side.

DVD-audio is a second-generation DIGITAL music format that provides even better quality than audio CDs.

DVD-ROM is like a large CD-ROM

DVD-RAM is a rewritable DVD that functions like an external DISK DRIVE. It can be rewritten about 100,000 times.

DVD-R and DVD+R are competing WORM DISK formats used to record movies or data. DVD-RW and DVD+RW are competing, rewritable formats that are only good for about 1,000 re-writes.

DVD drives in computers are more often than not combination DVD/CD players/recorders. *See also* CD-ROM DRIVE; DISK BURNING.

digitize
To convert text, images or sounds into a series of dots that can be read by a COMPUTER. It is also the term used to describe the process of scanning (*see* SCANNER).

DIMM (Double Inline Memory Module)
A small CIRCUIT BOARD containing RAM chips that increase the amount of memory available to a computer. (*See also* SIMM).

dip switch (Dual In-line Package switch)
One of a collection of small "on" and "off" switches used to select options on a CIRCUIT BOARD without having to modify the hardware. They are frequently found inside printers to control vertical spacing and other variable functions, and in computers and other electronic devices. A dip switch is the complete unit of plastic that contains the circuit and leads for fitting into the device. *See also* IRQ.

directory
The TABLE OF CONTENTS of a computer file SYSTEM that allows convenient access to specific files. A directory is an area of the DISK that stores files. It is common practice to store the files from one particular APPLICATION in a

directory structure

specific directory so that they do not get mixed up with other files. Files can then be recognized by their NAMES. When a directory is called up on screen it usually provides several items of information. Depending upon the settings chosen, the directory can indicate file size, when last used, type of file and in addition, the DIRECTORY STRUCTURE and location of each file is plain to see. In the illustration shown, double-clicking on the folder ICON on the left opens and expands it to show what it contains and this is displayed in the right-hand window. *See also* EXPLORER.

directory structure
see TREE STRUCTURE.

directory tree
see TREE STRUCTURE.

disk
see FLOPPY DISK; HARD DISK; CD ROM; DVD.

disk burning
The process of physically recording (or writing) DATA to a an OPTICAL DISK, so-called because it is done by a laser. However, there are some other storage devices, e.g. FLASH MEMORY or EPROM, to which data can be burned and subsequently erased or rewritten. *See also* CD BURNING; CD-ROM; CD-R/CD-RW; DUAL-PLATFORM DISK; DVD; PERIPHERAL; STORAGE DEVICE; WRITER.

disk cache
An area of computer RAM that is used as a temporary STORAGE for frequently-used DATA. It allows faster access

dithering

to the data than if the data were held on a PHYSICAL DISK. It therefore speeds up processing.

disk drive
The HARDWARE that enables information to be read from, and written to, a DISK. The recording and erasing is performed by the READ/WRITE HEAD. The circuitry controlling the drive is called the *disk drive controller*.

display
Synonymous with MONITOR; VIDEO DISPLAY UNIT.

To produce or provide an image. *See* IMAGING.

Also, a typographical term for the large-sized FONTS used in headlines, and particularly in advertisements. *See* DESKTOP PUBLISHING.

distributed computing *or* distributed service
The use of multiple computers networked throughout a very wide geographical area, whether through a dedicated network, or via the Internet. Often, this is done as part of a project or problem-solving exercise, e.g. SETI. It is also another way to describe file sharing services. *See also* peer-to-peer.

dithering
To combine small dots of different colors or shades to produce the effect of a new color or shade. For example, the combination of blue dots and yellow dots produces a green image. If the dots of blue are slightly larger than the yellow dots the shade of green becomes darker and moves towards purple. Use of dithering and a PALETTE of 256 colors can produce a continuously variable color range. *See also* COLOR REPRODUCTION.

DLL (Dynamic Link Library)

DLL (Dynamic Link Library)

An EXECUTABLE PROGRAM module in Windows. DLLs are launched by an executable program or by other DLLs. The WINDOWS operating system contains a huge number of DLLs, but each DLL can be shared by all running APPLICATIONS. DLLs can also be created for a particular application. DLL CONFLICTS are a source of trouble on Windows systems, although 2000 and XP have improved matters considerably.

DNS

see DOMAIN NAME SYSTEM *or* SERVER.

docking station

A HARDWARE device into which a NOTEBOOK COMPUTER can be connected to provide added facilities such as DISK DRIVE, CD ROM, color VDU, PRINTER access, etc. The notebook computer can easily be inserted and extracted from the docking station.

document

Traditionally, a piece of work created in a word processing program such as a letter, memo or report. Recently the term has been expanded to include work created in a DATABASE MANAGEMENT PROGRAM or SPREADSHEET.

document exchange software

SOFTWARE that allows such files to be viewed on computers that do not have the original APPLICATION installed. Usually, the software comprises a converter, which turns the document into a file recognized by the READER. The reader is generally available separately, for free.

Unlike FILE VIEWERS, document exchange applications have integral fonts and can also embed the fonts. The exchange file is, therefore, not dissimilar to an EPS. The reader may allow an element of editing or copying of the document content. *See also* ADOBE ACROBAT; EMBEDDING; PDF.

document object model (DOM)
A STANDARD from the W3C that defines a specification for an INTERFACE that allows a BROWSER to update the content, structure and style of HTML and XML documents. *See* DHTML.

document reader
A hardware DEVICE that scans printed text, converting the text into DIGITAL signals. Software converts the digitized files into readable text that can be edited as any WORD PROCESSING document. (*See also* SCANNER; OPTICAL CHARACTER RECOGNITION; SPEECH RECOGNITION.)

document type definition (DTD)
Defines what TAGS and ATTRIBUTES are used to describe the content of an SGML or XML document. A BROWSER will use a DTD to read and display the document's contents. DTD definitions may be embedded within a document or in a separate file. Note that a DTD does not in itself define the content – this is done (in XML) by a SCHEMA. *See also* XSD.

documentation
Books that provide information and instruction in the use of a piece of hardware or software. Since the books are bulky and expensive to print some manufacturers provide

DOM

the information on disk. The information can be accessed as a TUTORIAL file or often as part of an ONLINE HELP system.

DOM
see DOCUMENT OBJECT MODEL.

domain name
Most commonly used to mean the name referring to an Internet site, service or computer and in the main representing a business or an organization. The full name consists of several parts; from the left is the identifying name followed by the @ sign and then the subdomain name (which will be the Internet service provider). This is followed by the domain type (such as com, co, org, etc.) and then the country code.

domain name system *or* server (DNS)
An Internet service that translates domain names into IP addresses. Every time you use a domain name, therefore, a DNS service must translate the name into the corresponding IP address. For example, the domain name www.cheapskate.com might translate into 238.908.657.2. *See also* URL.

domain type
This is another part of an address which indicates what sort of organization is involved. The system has recently changed but some types are:

com	company
org	non-profit organization
edu	educational institution
ac	academic (in the UK)
gov	government body

dongle
A COPY PROTECTION device that plugs into a PORT on a PC. Software sends a code to that port, and the key responds with its serial number, which verifies its presence to the program. The key therefore hinders software duplication, because each copy of the program is tied to the unique dongle number. Also called a *hardware key*.

DOS (Disk Operating System)
The program responsible for communications between a computer and its PERIPHERAL DEVICES such as the DISK DRIVE, PRINTER or the VDU. It controls and manages all the peripheral devices connected to the computer system. It therefore must be the first program to be loaded when the computer is switched on. The commonest OPERATING SYSTEM is MS-DOS (produced by Microsoft Corporation in the USA), which was introduced in 1981.

dot matrix printer
A piece of equipment for printing characters. It is an IMPACT PRINTER, and as such is comparatively noisy when compared to non-impact printers such as INKJET or LASER, which have superseded dot matrix printers.

dot pitch
A measure of the RESOLUTION of computer screens or printers. The smaller the dot pitch the sharper the image that is displayed. A dot pitch of 0.28mm is HIGH RESOLUTION while 0.4mm is LOW RESOLUTION.

dots per inch (dpi)
A measure of the RESOLUTION of a screen or printer. The

double density disk

more dots per inch that the computer can display or print the higher the resolution. (*See also* DOT PITCH).

double density disk

A FLOPPY DISK that can store approximately 2 megabytes of data.

double inline memory module
See DIMM.

double-click

To click the mouse button twice in quick succession. A control panel utility can be used to set the time delay between clicks of the mouse. A double-click can extend the use of the single click. For example, a single click positions the cursor in a word while double-clicking selects the whole word. Single clicking on a program icon selects the icon while double clicking will select the icon and open the program. A file can similarly be selected with a double click.

double-sided disk

A type of FLOPPY DISK with both surfaces available for storage of data. Two READ/WRITE HEADS are required for double-sided disks.

down time

The time when computer equipment is not available for use because of hardware or software malfunction.

download

To copy a file from an online information service or from another computer to your computer. It is the opposite

drag and drop

of upload, and is particularly common with users of the Internet. Programs, upgrades, games, demonstrations, etc. can all be downloaded by clicking on the appropriate button. The rate of progress is then shown on screen and the transfer rate given. The time taken to download depends on the size of the file, the modem and speed of the network.

downstream
Transmission from the provider to an end user. It could be a signal transmitted from a SERVER to a WORKSTATION across a NETWORK, or the downloading of files to a customer. Transmission from end user to provider is called UPSTREAM.

dpi
see DOTS PER INCH.

draft mode
The quickest, LOW RESOLUTION output from a DOT MATRIX or INKJET PRINTER. It is used to produce a document used for initial review and editing prior to producing the final full quality output.

drag
To hold down the mouse button and move the mouse pointer across the screen. The drag technique is used to select an area of text in a word processing document or to select a group of cells in a spreadsheet or to select a group of document icons in a desk top window.

drag and drop
Having selected an area of text (for example, in a word

processing document) with the drag command, the selection can be dragged from one part of the document to another and then dropped into its new place in the document.

DRAM (Dynamic RAM)

A type of computer memory chip that cannot retain memory and so has to be continually refreshed (*see* REFRESH). This type of chip is used to transfer data within the computer.

draw program

A GRAPHICS application used for creating and editing images, where the image is represented by VECTOR GRAPHICS, which allows all elements of the picture to be isolated, moved and scaled independently.
CAD programs are similar, but draw programs provide a large number of special effects and editing TOOLS. Images that have been created with a draw program can be adjusted to any RESOLUTION for output.
A commonly known example of such a program is CorelDraw. *See also* OBJECT ORIENTED GRAPHICS; PAINT PROGRAM.

drive

An electromechanical device that spins disks and tapes at a specified speed.
Also, to provide power to a DEVICE or PROGRAM, or the means by which such can operate.

driver

A file containing information which allows a program to control and operate a PERIPHERAL device (such as a printer, scanner or monitor). Also called a DEVICE DRIVER. When a new item is connected to a computer, the driver is installed so that the item can operate.

drop down menu
A list of command options that appears only when the main command is selected. Use of drop down menus allows programmers to provide many options to the user without cluttering the screen.

drum scanner
see SCANNER.

DSL (Digital Subscriber Line)
The two main types are ADSL and SDSL. DSL technologies pack large quantities of data onto copper wires. They are sometimes referred to as *last-mile technologies*, because they are used only for connecting from a telephone exchange to a user. *See also* BROADBAND.

DSP (Digital Signal Processor)
A COPROCESSOR that manipulates ANALOG information, such as audio or an image, that has been DIGITIZED. *See* DIGITAL CAMERA.

DTD
see DOCUMENT TYPE DEFINITION.

DTP
see DESKTOP PUBLISHING.

dual-platform disk
Commonly, a CD-ROM containing DATA that can be

dumb terminal

accessed by both Windows and Macintosh operating systems.

Although, of recent years, there has been increasing ease of use between the two formats, it is particularly important in the case of ROM STORAGE DEVICES that the data is presented in a matching FORMAT.

One way to do this is by using an APPLICATION called Toast, on a Macintosh, where a blank CD-ROM is partitioned, and each PARTITION is formatted appropriately. Each partitioned area is known as a VOLUME and is essentially a LOGICAL DRIVE, and carries either Mac or Windows formatted data. It is possible for data on the disk to be shared between the volumes, regardless of which format this data is in. *See also* CD BURNING; CD-ROM DRIVE.

dumb terminal
A computer terminal that lacks its own CENTRAL PROCESSING UNIT and DISK DRIVES.

dump
The process of transferring the contents of memory in one storage device to another storage device or item of hardware. For example, it may be a dump from disk to printer, disk to tape or screen to printer. Dumps are often performed when programmers are debugging programs (*see* DEBUG).

DUN
See DIAL-UP NETWORKING.

duplex
see FULL DUPLEX.

dynamic HTML (DHTML)

DVD
see DIGITAL VIDEO/VERSATILE DISC.

DVI (Digital Video Interface)
A set of standards or specifications for combining conventional computer techniques with those of video.

Dvorak keyboard
An alternative KEYBOARD from the normal QWERTY keyboard. Some 70 per cent of the keystrokes are made on the home row compared with around 30 per cent with the QWERTY layout.

dynamic content
WEBSITE content that changes, e.g. on a site providing current stocks and shares prices, or one providing live news. *See* DHTML.

dynamic data exchange
An interprocess channel through which correctly-prepared programs can exchange data and control other programs.

dynamic font
see EMBEDDED FONT.

dynamic HTML (DHTML)
Coding that creates WEB PAGES that are changeable, dependent on the viewer, e.g. pages that display search results, the time of day, or locally relevant information.

They are created using a combination of HTML, CSS, CGI, COOKIES, and scripting languages such as

dynamic link

JAVASCRIPT. Dynamic HTML is integrated with the DOCUMENT OBJECT MODEL developed by the W3C.

dynamic link

A method of linking data shared by two separate programs. When data is changed by one program it is changed immediately for use by the other. This type of link is required in MULTIUSER networks.

dynamic web page

A WEB PAGE that provides DYNAMIC CONTENT. *See* DHTML.

E

e-business
Often synonymous with E-COMMERCE, but actually more of an overall term for having a business presence on the web. An e-business may offer more than just selling its products and services.

echo
To show on screen the commands being executed by a computer as they are being performed.

e-commerce (or electronic commerce)
Making online business transactions, or buying products or services online, is increasing in scope and popularity. Companies see the Internet as the new frontier, a potentially low-cost route to gaining sales in a global marketplace.

edit
To change or alter text, graphics or values that appear in a file. The edit process is required to correct mistakes previously made in a file and is a core function of all word processing software.

edutainment
The growing selection of computer software that educates the user while being entertaining.

EGA (Enhanced Graphic Adapter)
A color bit-mapped (*see* BITMAP) VDU display adapter for IBM-compatible PERSONAL COMPUTERS. It displays up to

e-journal

16 colors simultaneously with a RESOLUTION of 640 x 350 PIXELS.

e-journal
An online publication which can be accessed on the web, commonly used in the academic world.

electronic marketplace
Every day more businesses are offering their goods and services for sale over the INTERNET. Payment for goods or services in this electronic marketplace is made by credit card and goods are shipped by courier as in normal mail order.

electronic publishing
The use of the INTERNET to publish and distribute work, online news services, online encyclopedia or computer-based training manuals, etc. The term may also include the publication of material, whether text, DATABASES or other type of information, on CD-ROM or FLOPPY DISK. *See also* INTERNET PUBLISHING.

email
The use of a network of computers to send and receive messages. Email is now used extensively for personal, business, or educational purposes, virtually instantaneously. Files sent with emails are known as ATTACHMENTS.

email attachment
see ATTACHMENT

embedded computer
see EMBEDDED SYSTEM.

embedding

embedded font
A FONT that has been placed into a DOCUMENT such that all of the DATA about the font is available *within* the document, so that when the document is viewed on another computer, the fonts will be properly displayed, regardless of whether that computer actually has those fonts installed or not. Microsoft undertook a lot of work in this field in the 1990s, in concert with Adobe, particularly with regard to WEB PAGES, in the form of Microsoft Font Embedding, and also produced Embedded Open Type. *See also* ADOBE ACROBAT; CSS; HTML; OLE; TRUETYPE; POSTSCRIPT; XML.

embedded system
Any SYSTEM with a CPU, but which cannot be defined as a COMPUTER. Vast numbers of consumer products, tools, systems and other hardware can be described as embedded systems. The PROCESSOR may be proprietary ware or custom-made. They are used in automobiles, planes, trains, cameras, consumer and office appliances, mobile phones, PDAs and other HANDHELDS, as well as in manufacturing itself. The list is endless.

In such systems, the SOFTWARE is stored in READ ONLY MEMORY. Sometimes, if the system is relatively complex, e.g. a bench tool controller, it may be known as an *embedded computer*. *See also* CAD/CAM; RAPID PROTOTYPING.

embedding
To place an OBJECT created by one APPLICATION into a DOCUMENT created by another, such that the object is still active, or dynamic, and retains its FORMAT. Contrast with *pasting*, wherein the object so placed becomes a static part of the second document. *See also* ADOBE ACROBAT; EMBEDDED FONT; OLE.

emoticon

emoticon
An ICON representing emotion (hence the name) made up of standard keyboard characters. Many of them are viewed sideways and although there are several hundred, some are more obvious than others. A few examples are:
:)   smiling face
:-) smile
:-D big smile
Emoticons are also called *smileys*.

emulate
To duplicate the function of a program, operating system or hardware device in another computer system.

Encapsulated PostScript
see EPS

encryption
The method of encoding data so that unauthorized users cannot read or otherwise use the data. Data can be jumbled by a computer program, communicated to another computer and, as long as the receiving computer has the same encryption program, recompiled into meaningful information.

enhanced parallel port
A parallel PORT standard that supports BIDIRECTIONAL communication. EPP is about 10 times faster than the older Centronics standard and can communicate with all sorts of PERIPHERALS.

environment
The style or setting in which the user enters

erase

commands into or performs tasks with the computer. The GRAPHICAL USER INTERFACES provide an environment or setting that looks similar to a desktop while a DOS system provides a command line environment.

EPP
see ENHANCED PARALLEL PORT.

EPROM (Erasable Programmable Read Only Memory)
A memory CHIP that can be programmed, erased and reprogrammed.

EPS (Encapsulated PostScript)
The GRAPHICS file format used by the PostScript language. EPS files contain a bitmapped representation of an image, rather than just the PostScript commands for printing it. Typically, it might be used to IMPORT an image created in an IMAGE EDITOR into a PAGE LAYOUT PROGRAM document. The document and embedded EPS image would be saved in the native file format of the program (e.g. PageMaker). *See also* DRAW PROGRAM; EMBEDDING; VECTOR GRAPHICS.

erasable storage
A READ/WRITE secondary storage device in which data can be written and erased repeatedly. A HARD DISK is such a device whereas a CD ROM is not since it cannot be erased once data is written to it.

erase
To rub out or delete from a STORAGE device.

error message

A message displayed on a screen that indicates that the computer has detected an error or malfunction. *error trapping* is the ability of a program to recognize and almost anticipate an error and then carry out a pre-set course of action in response to the error. *See also* WEB SERVER ERROR MESSAGE.

escape key (esc)

A nonprinting character or keyboard control key that causes an interruption in the normal program sequence. Within a software program it is usually pressed to cancel a command or operation.

Ethernet

A local area network (LAN) hardware standard capable of linking up to 1,024 computers in a network, and it is the most common LAN method used. It was developed by Digital, Intel and Xerox. Ethernet can transfer up to 10 megabits per second and Fast Ethernet operates at 100 megabits per second. The Ethernet hub is a unit into which all the computers are linked.

EtherTalk

An implementation of the ETHERNET local area network developed by APPLE and the 3com corporation, designed to work with the APPLESHARE network system.

event-driven program

A program that is constructed to react to the computer user who initiates events such as clicking a mouse rather than a COMMAND-driven program, which requires specific commands to be typed into the computer to obtain results.

executable program *or* executable file
A PROGRAM file that is ready to run, often seen as the "main" file of an APPLICATION (amongst the others, data, text and document files). In DOS, executable files have an EXE EXTENSION.

execute
To carry out the individual steps called for by the program in a computer.

expanded type
A TYPE STYLE where the spacing between the characters and the width of the characters themselves has been expanded, or stretched, so that the CPI decreases. *See also* CONDENSED TYPE; KERN.

expansion bus
see BUS.

expansion card
A printed CIRCUIT BOARD that is fitted into the main computer board. Expansion boards are fitted to enhance the power of the computer, providing facilities such as MODEMS, added memory and high speed graphics.

expansion slot
A PORT in the main computer system that allows the fitting of an expansion card. There are several slots available for fitting expansion cards in computers.

expert system
A program that uses the accumulated expertise in a

Explorer

specific area of many people in order to assist non-experts who wish to solve problems.

Explorer
The file manager utility that comes with Windows and which shows the directories/folders, files and other information about a computer's disks.

export
To create a data file in one program that can be transferred to another computer and be read by another program. Exported files can usually be transferred in a particular format to ensure that they can be read in the new system.

extended memory specification
see XMS.

extensible log format
A standard that defines the FORMAT of WEBLOG files, the aim being the standardization of weblog file formats on an XML-based standard. *See also* MARKUP LANGUAGE; XML.

extensible markup language
see XML.

extension (*see also* file name)
All files usually possess a set of three characters after the file name proper. In many programs this extension is appended automatically, although it is not absolutely necessary. However, it helps in recognizing the file type and import filters may not automatically import a file if there is no extension or if it is not recognized.

F

FAQ (Frequently Asked Question(s))
Newsgroups and other sites have FAQ documents on various topics. As the name implies, FAQs contain a lot of useful information giving hints and answers to common questions. It is also the first level in any online customer service, technical support or other troubleshooting system.

FAT
see FILE ALLOCATION TABLE.

FAT32
The 32-bit version of the FILE ALLOCATION TABLE system. FAT32 was introduced in 1996. It supports larger disk partitions and file sizes and has more safeguards than the earlier FAT.

favorites
The Microsoft Internet Explorer equivalent to Bookmarks in Netscape Navigator. It enables the user to build up a list of frequently visited sites. While visiting a particular site, it can be added to the Favorites list simply by clicking on the menu and selecting "Add to Favorites." Thereafter the chosen site can be accessed simply by clicking on the name given to it on the Favorites list.

fax or fax machine or facsimile
A device capable of transmitting or receiving an exact copy of a page of printed or pictorial matter over

feed

telephone lines. To transmit, the original document is fed into the machine, where it is scanned by a mirror-and-lens-aided device, or, in some faxes, by a series of light-emitting diodes (LEDs). Light and dark picture elements – PIXELS – are described digitally, and the message is shortened by compressing much of the white space. The receiving machine, which is addressed through its telephone number, translates the code it receives back into a pattern of grays, black and white. The reconstituted message is printed out using techniques similar to those of photocopying machines.

feed

The process of supplying paper to a printer. Paper can be fed into the printer either by a friction system or a TRACTOR FEED device, which gives *line feed* when the printer moves the paper forward one line at a time. Laser printers use *page feed*, which ejects one page at a time. (*See also* SHEET FEEDER.)

fiber optics

A method of carrying information along cables using light. This method of transmitting data is faster and more reliable than conventional wires. Recent developments have allowed scientists to pass an amount of information equivalent to 1000 bibles per second along a fiber optic cable.

field

A defined group of characters or numbers, e.g. a customer number, a product description, a telephone number or address within a specific space in a DATABASE program.

file

A collection of data that is given a distinct name and is stored on the computer's SECONDARY STORAGE. Files are stored within directories, analogous to the old system of filing cabinet, drawers and folders.

file allocation table (FAT)

A table held on a computer disk that keeps a record of the location on a disk of all the files. Files can be distributed in many locations on a disk, and the FAT keeps a record of the locations so that the file appears contiguous, or in one piece, to the user.

file association

A link between a document file and the program that created it so that when a document file is selected by double clicking it opens the program and hence the file. Without file association, double clicking the document would have no effect.

file attribute

information held in a file directory that contains details about the file and how the computer can access it.

file compression

The process of condensing a file with the result that it takes up around half the normal space on a disk. The effective transmission speed can be increased by around a factor of four by using data compression. Data compression essentially involves the substitution of longer, recognizable strings of characters by shorter ones (for example, one character replacing the word "the" every time it occurs). This and other substitutions are

file compression utility

recorded in a table which is also held by the person to whom the file is sent where the original characters are restored, and the file reverts to its full size.

file compression utility

A program that is designed to compress files. There are various programs available that will compress files, e.g. Stuffit, Disk Doubler and JPEG for graphics. (*See also* FILE COMPRESSION). Compressed files can be recognized by their file extension and can only be opened by the appropriate program. There are many such programs, including PKZIP and WinZip. Versions for the Mac include UnZip and Stuffit.

file conversion

with the interchange and distribution of files between computers, individuals and companies, files created in one program have to be converted into a different program or version of the same program. Major word processing applications of a compatible generation can accept files from each other, using built-in filters. Stand alone programs perform this function, such as Conversions Plus. These can open a file and save it to one of a number of different formats.

file conversion utility

A program that is designed to convert files created in one program for use by another program. For example, files created in Word can be converted and used by Word Perfect.

file extension

see FILE NAME.

file sharing

file format
The method that an OPERATING SYSTEM or program uses to store data on a disk. Different software companies have different methods of storing data, with the result that it is difficult for one program to read a file created in another program. (*See also* FILE CONVERSION UTILITY).

file manager
A utility program that allows the user to copy, delete, add or move files around without reverting to the DOS commands and to create directories. Microsoft Windows uses a file manager program to assist its users.

file name
A name given to a file by the computer user so that the operating system recognizes the file. Every file on a disk directory must have a distinct name.

file recovery
The process of retrieving or restoring a file that has been previously erased.

file server
A COMPUTER in a network that provides access to the storage media for workstations or other computers in the network. The operation of the network operating system ensures a seamless view of the server's files from each workstation. The server is usually a high-powered computer with a very large storage capacity that is set aside as the controller for the clients on the network. (*See also* SERVER.)

file sharing
The crux of a PEER-TO-PEER NETWORK. Files are made

file transfer protocol (FTP)

sharable on a computer (in the network settings MENU area), so that the other computers in the network can also read (and copy) the files (but not WRITE TO). When file sharing is done over the Internet, it is often known as *swapping*.

One well-known service is KaZaA, which distributes its directories of files to the user's own computer. The computer then communicates with other users' computers to complete a search. Files are then downloaded "in pieces" from multiple other users and "reassembled". During this process, other users may start downloading the same files to their computers, and so on. This can take time, and it also uses up processing power and BANDWIDTH.

Napster, on the other hand, provided a central index to files in other people's computers. Only whole files were transmitted from one user to another.

The trouble with all of these services is that they allow you to access any bunch of files pretty much for free, and the most popular type of file often ends up being material that is copyrighted. Napster was originally set up with the sole aim of sharing music audio files. This was seen as breach of copyright by the publishers. In the end, Napster was closed down (although it has been relaunched as a subscription/fee DOWNLOAD service).

Another sometimes troublesome aspect of these services is that they usually download some SPYWARE onto your system.

file transfer protocol (FTP)
A standard that controls ASYNCHRONOUS COMMUNICATIONS by telephone to ensure error-free transmission of files. *See* FTP.

file viewer
SOFTWARE that displays the contents of a FILE as it would be displayed by the APPLICATION that created it. *See also* DOCUMENT EXCHANGE SOFTWARE; GRAPHICS VIEWER.

fill
An operation that is used in a SPREADSHEET program to enter values in a range of CELLS. For example, a range of dates can be "filled" into cells to act as headings for a monthly cash flow report.

filter
To select certain files from a DATABASE by setting up a set of criteria.

finder
A UTILITY PROGRAM that manages memory and files in conjunction with the Macintosh operating system.

firewall
A combination of HARDWARE and SOFTWARE that prevents unauthorized access to a NETWORK. Firewalls can be present in both hardware and software, or a combination of the two. They are often used to prevent people from accessing PRIVATE NETWORKS (like intranets) that are connected to the Internet. In practice, many firewalls have default settings that provide little or no security unless specific actions are taken by the owner.

Hardware firewalls are generally utilized in network components (including routers). However, software firewalls are also available to protect individual workstations from attack. *See also* CRACK; HACKER; ENCRYPTION; INTRANET; ROUTER.

Firewire

Firewire
High-speed serial BUS that allows the connection of up to 63 DEVICES. It was intended for downloading DIGITAL VIDEO and also for handling complex MULTIMEDIA files, but is now becoming popular for, e.g. direct computer connections. FireWire supports HOT SWAPPING, and is extremely fast.

firmware
The part of the system software that is stored permanently in the computer's read only memory (*see* ROM). Firmware cannot be altered or modified.

fixed disk
see HARD DISK.

Flash
A widely used VECTOR-GRAPHICS animation technology from Macromedia. As long as browsers are equipped with the necessary plug-ins, Flash animations will always look the same.

flash memory
A type of memory device that can be programmed, erased and reprogrammed. It is retained when the power is turned off. Flash memory cards, similar in size to credit cards, are used to store programs and files for PERSONAL DIGITAL ASSISTANTS, LAPTOP COMPUTERS and NOTEBOOK COMPUTERS where size and space-saving are crucial.

flat file
Database a DATABASE MANAGEMENT PROGRAM that can

access only one record or file at a time. This restricts the usefulness of the program compared with a RELATIONAL DATABASE management program.

flat shading
In computer GRAPHICS, to add a shaded surface to an object in order to simulate simple lighting. *See also* GOURAUD SHADING; PHONG SHADING; RENDER.

flatbed scanner
A hardware device that is used to transfer text and graphics from paper into a digitized format that can then be edited in a computer program. (*See also* OPTICAL CHARACTER RECOGNITION).

flicker
A distortion that occurs on a VDU, caused by a low rate of refreshment of the screen, i.e. the electron beam does not progress over the screen fast enough to reflect changes in the display when the display is constantly changing.

floating point calculation
A form of calculation that the computer employs for calculating numbers. The decimal point in a number is not fixed but floats, allowing a high level of accuracy in calculations. The floating point calculation in some programs can handle numbers up to 1020 accurately. Other programs, however, may effectively limit the accuracy of a calculation by reducing the size of the numbers to, say, 1015.

floppy disk
A removable secondary medium of storage for computers.

floptical disk

The disks, usually 31/2 inch, are made of a plastic that is coated with magnetic material (of which the main component is ferric oxide); the whole thing is protected by a rigid plastic cover. The disk rotates within its cover, and an access hole allows the READ/WRITE HEAD of the disk drive to record and retrieve information. There is a WRITE-PROTECT notch on the disk cover that can be set so that the disk drive cannot change the disk but can only read the data stored there. Floppy disks are still used as a means of installing software, backing up files and transferring data between users, though they are being overtaken by CDs, Zips etc.

floptical disk

A FLOPPY DISK that, because of its construction, allows the disk drive's READ/WRITE HEADS to align very accurately with the disk. This allows a far greater amount of information to be stored on a disk.

flow

when data is being imported into a word processing document or page layout document, the imported text will flow into the available columns and around any graphic images. When one column is filled the text will flow into the next column.

folder

In GRAPHICAL USER INTERFACE systems a folder is the DIRECTORY in which files are located or stored. The folder is represented on screen by an ICON styled like a physical folder in a filing cabinet.

font

A complete set of letters, numbers, special characters

and punctuation marks of a particular size and for one identifiable typeface whether roman or bold (the WEIGHT), italic or upright (the posture). The term is often used to refer to a family of fonts or TYPEFACES, although this is technically incorrect. Fonts come as bit-mapped (*see* BITMAP) or OUTLINE FONTS.

font family
A set of FONTS sharing the same TYPEFACE but differing in the size and the boldness of the type.

font incompatibility
In DOCUMENT exchange, errors in the layout of a document caused by a difference between the installed FONTS in the computer used to create the document and those in the computer used to display or print that document. Without having exactly the same fonts installed, a document will display differently, or with errors, on another computer. This is why the same small set of fonts tend to be used over and over. EMBEDDING the fonts from the source computer into the document solves the problem, and is a core aspect of ADOBE ACROBAT. The reason why an application might display another font instead is because it allows FONT SUBSTITUTION (which is something Acrobat does, too). Experienced users sometimes get over this by attaching the relevant font files to the document. In HTML, font substitution is provided by specifying alternatives in the font TAG. *See also* DOCUMENT EXCHANGE SOFTWARE; PDF.

font substitution
In document exchange, when FONT INCOMPATIBILITY arises, some applications will substitute a FONT that most

closely approximates the missing font. This still depends upon which fonts the computer has installed, and can therefore be somewhat "hit and miss", leading to document errors or incorrect display. ADOBE ACROBAT is able to carry out very precise font substitution from its own integral fonts, if it is unable to embed the fonts of the original when making a PDF.

One solution is to stick with fonts that will almost certainly be available, such as Times Roman; another (in HTML) is to specify several alternatives; yet another is to use TEXT GRAPHICS FILE. The WORLDWIDE WEB CONSORTIUM has developed a standard whereby fonts can be embedded into a WEB PAGE using CASCADING STYLE SHEETS and SCALABLE VECTOR GRAPHICS. *See also* DOCUMENT EXCHANGE SOFTWARE; EMBEDDING.

footer

Text positioned at the foot of a page by a word processing program, for example. The type of text could vary from the file name, date, time, page number, originator or other relevant text.

footnote

A note at the bottom of a page in a word processing or page layout document that is used to explain a word or phrase or concept. The word being footnoted is identified by the placement of a superscripted number after the word. This number corresponds to the footnote number.

footprint

A physical measure of the amount of desk space that a computer and its peripheral devices take up when sitting

formatting

on the user's desk. If the computer footprint takes up the whole desktop space there is no room left to work.

forecasting
A method of using past results to project results into the future. For example, future sales can be forecast by analyzing the results of past months and years.

foreground task
The priority job that the computer is undertaking in precedence to the other tasks that are being processed in the BACKGROUND. The foreground task is the task that you are monitoring on the computer screen. To support foreground and background processing the computer must be capable of MULTITASKING.

format
The structure (or layout) of an item, whether it be a text DOCUMENT, a DATABASE record, or a computer SYSTEM; the structure (or type) of PROGRAM and DATA files – EXECUTABLE PROGRAMS, WORD PROCESSING documents, GRAPHICS FILES and databases, for example.

The arrangement or organization of data, established by the APPLICATION that created (organized) the file, which must be read by the same (or a similar) program so that the data can be interpreted and presented. See FILE FORMAT.

To initialize a STORAGE medium (e.g. HARD DISK) to hold data.

See also EXTENSION; FILE VIEWER.

formatting
The process of instruction that produces the desired

formula

format of text in a document for on-screen display or printing.

formula

A calculation in a program, such as a SPREADSHEET, that defines a relationship between values that can be directly input or are already present in the spreadsheet.

FORTRAN (FORmula TRANslation)

A HIGH-LEVEL PROGRAMMING LANGUAGE designed for mathematical, engineering and scientific work. It was developed in the 1950s by IBM.

forum

A designated group in which discussion takes place via the electronic network. ONLINE INFORMATION SERVICE providers set up resources to allow people to choose from a wide range of subjects or to choose a general area where any subject can be discussed (subject to the rules of the service provider).

See also CHAT FORUM.

404

Someone who is generally uninformed or clueless. From the WEB SERVER ERROR MESSAGE "Not found".

fractals

Groups of shapes that are alike but not identical, such as leaves or snowflakes. No two snowflakes are identical but they have generally similar patterns. Computer programs can create fractals to provide artists and designers with a huge variety of graphic images.

fragmentation

The storage of files on a disk that uses non-contiguous sectors to store the file. On a newly formatted disk, a file will be stored in its entirety in one location. The next file to be stored will take up the next sectors, and so on until the disk is full. When several files are deleted the relevant sectors are free for new storage of files, but one sector may not be large enough for a file. The process of saving and deleting files will result in a particular file being located in many sectors on the disk. Disks can be defragmented using a utility program.

free form database

A form of DATABASE that has no preset structure of information on each record. The information that can be held on one record can be completely different from the information on another record. Such free form databases are useful for storing general notes that are accumulated on a desk notepad, for example.

freeware

Copyrighted programs that are provided by the author free of charge. These programs may not have been fully tested, resulting in errors or system crashes, or they may carry a computer VIRUS. Nevertheless, they do have their uses. Many software companies provide at least some form of freeware product. ADOBE READER is freeware, for instance.

frequency

A measure of the speed at which a computer processor operates. It is measured in MEGAHERTZ.

front end

front end
The starting point for a user of a SYSTEM or APPLICATION; the point where primary inputs are made; the client side of a CLIENT/SERVER application; the USER INTERFACE. See also GUI.

front office
Refers to the parts of a commercial NETWORK that provide for an interface with a customer. Also the SOFTWARE that the customer interfaces with, e.g. a "shopping basket". Areas of business such applications cover include ordering, customer service and customer support. Generally, such a system needs a BACK OFFICE, too. *See also* CLIENT/SERVER.

FST (Flatter Squarer Tube)
The technology for producing a VDU or TV screen that is flat rather than having the traditional convex surface.

FTP (File Transfer Protocol)
A protocol used for moving files over a network such as the Internet. The protocol includes the means to access the network, examine directories, and copy files. This is undertaken by an FTP utility running within the application. An anonymous FTP site or directory holds files that anyone can download. However, the use of browsers on the Internet to find appropriate web pages from which files can be downloaded is now more common than specific searches of FTP sites.

full backup utility
A utility program that creates a full backup of the files on a disk. It is different from an INCREMENTAL BACKUP,

which backs up only the files that have been altered since the previous backup.

full duplex
A protocol for ASYNCHRONOUS COMMUNICATIONS, which allows the sending and receiving of signals at the same time. Asynchronous communication requires the correct standard of cabling.

function
Any single operation of a computer or word processor, e.g. editing. Also, within certain programs such as SPREADSHEETS, a procedure that is stored in the program and that will perform a particular sequence of operations or calculations to produce an end result.

function key
A key on the keyboard of a word processor or computer system that enables the user to perform a particular task or execute a command that might otherwise take several keystrokes.

fuzzy logic
A description of the development away from strict logical arguments to take account of human or non-logical behavior. The development of ARTIFICIAL INTELLIGENCE requires a degree of fuzzy logic since human decisions are rarely based on strict rules of logic.

G

gateway
A device that converts communications from one PROTOCOL or BANDWIDTH to another. This function allows two different types of NETWORK to communicate with each other. For example a LOCAL AREA NETWORK (LAN) can communicate with a WIDE AREA NETWORK (WAN), and a LAN can be connected with the INTERNET.

geek
often used to refer to people who have an obsession with computers, programming and the Internet.

GIF (Graphics Interchange Format)
An efficient file compression system for graphic images (pictures). Because of its efficiency, GIF files are used widely for downloading from ONLINE services. It was developed by CompuServe and is a raster type of format. It uses 8-bit color, i.e. 256 colors and works by selecting the most representative colors in the image.

giga
A prefix meaning one billion (a thousand million), and abbreviated g.

gigabyte
One billion BYTES or 1,000 MEGABYTES, although, strictly speaking, a gigabyte is 1,073,741,824 bytes. Hard disk capacities of one gigabyte on PERSONAL COMPUTERS are increasingly common.

GIGO (Garbage In, Garbage Out)
A common situation where poor or distorted results from a program are caused by incorrect input or mistakes in the input. Thus the quality of the data output is only as good as the quality of the input.

GIS (Geographic Information System)
Often called *mapping software*, GIS links the attributes and characteristics of an area to its geographic location. It is used in a variety of applications, including exploration, demographics, tracking, and map making. Unlike paper maps, digital maps can be combined with layers of such information.

glare
The reflection of light from the computer screen. This can be very distracting and can cause stress if not corrected by using a glare filter or by moving the screen.

glitch
A malfunction caused by a hardware fault. The malfunction is most often caused by a power surge or interruption.

global
A style or format that is applied throughout a document or program. For example, all ruler settings in a word processing document can be set to the same tabs, etc. Similarly, all cells in a SPREADSHEET program can be set to the same numeric format.

global positioning system
see GPS.

glossary

glossary
In word processing documents, a glossary can be used to store phrases or styles that are commonly used. This saves time when keying in text as an abbreviation for the common phrase can be used and then automatically substituted.

gopher
A means of searching for files using a particular set of menus. At one point there were thousands of gopher servers on the Net and a significant number dealt with a specific subject or line of interest. Now there are few such servers, although it is still used in some circles to archive material. In some ways gopher services can be more useful than using the successor search engines such as AltaVista, Yahoo and so on, because of the enormous number of sometimes superfluous results they often produce.

goto
A programming phrase that directs the program logic to a part of the program in order to accomplish a specific function. Also, a command feature that allows the user to select a page to move to in a word processing document or allows the user to select a cell to go to in a SPREADSHEET program.

Gouraud shading
In computer GRAPHICS, a technique developed by Henri Gouraud. It is the simplest rendering method and does not produce shadows or reflections. *See also* FLAT SHADING; PHONG SHADING; RENDER.

graphical user interface (GUI)

GPS (Global Positioning System)
A worldwide satellite navigational system originally developed for military use. The GPS satellites continuously transmit digital radio signals. Based on this information, the receivers know how long it takes for the signal to reach the receiver. By using three satellites, GPS can calculate the longitude and latitude of the receiver. By using four satellites, GPS can also determine altitude.

grabber
A representation of the mouse pointer with which images, text or cells are selected by moving the pointer across the selection required.

grandparent
The oldest file in a grandparent, PARENT, son BACKUP system. The grandparent file should not need to be used unless both the parent and child backups have been used and corrupted.

graph
A pictorial representation of values that is used to show the relationships between the values. Graphs are an invaluable way of getting a message across. The old adage is "a picture paints a thousand words".

graphical user interface (GUI)
The part of the software program that communicates and interacts with the user by means of pull-down MENUS, DIALOG BOXES and ICONS. The GUI makes computers easier to use because people respond to graphic representations of concepts, etc, much more

graphics

readily than if they have to read words. Microsoft Windows and Microsoft OS use this system.

graphics

A generic term used to describe anything to do with pictures as opposed to text. There are two types of graphic images used by computer programs: OBJECT-ORIENTED PROGRAMS or draw programs and bit-mapped (*see* BITMAP) or PAINT PROGRAMS. Object-oriented programs are used where precision graphics are required, e.g. in CAD or architecture programs. Bit-mapped graphics are useful in artistic applications where shading and patterns are more important than precision.

graphics files

Programs dedicated to graphics work with a variety of file formats, importing files, modifying them and saving in the same or a new format, or exporting for another application. Two types of graphic are used, namely VECTOR or RASTER and some programs can use both and convert between them. Typical raster type (also called bitmaps) graphic formats are: TIFF (.TIF), Bitmaps (.BMP), CompuServe (.GIF), Joint Photographic Experts Group (.JPG), and PhotoCD (.PCD). Typical vector type graphic formats are: Adobe Illustrator (.AI), CorelDraw (.CDR), Corel Metafile Exchange (.CMX), Encapsulated PostScript (.PS), and Windows Metafile (.WMF).

graphics tablet

An input device that uses a touch sensitive pad and a stylus. The movement of the stylus over the tablet generates an electrical pulse that is recorded by the computer and translated into a digital form as a screen PIXEL. The drawing on the pad is thus transferred to the screen.

graphics viewer
An APPLICATION that displays GRAPHICS FILES, regardless of file format. Allowing images to be rapidly previewed and organized, there may also be some editing TOOLs. They also list file ATTRIBUTES, e.g. file size, RESOLUTION, etc.

gray scale
The shades of gray from white to black that a computer can display. The more gray scales that are used the more realistic the picture will look. However, memory and storage required increase with the number of gray scales used.

groupware
Software that enhances the productivity of a group of workers who may be using a local area network. Groupware systems cater for sharing of documents, management of documents, scheduling facilities, and conferencing. It provides an effective system of communication which carries messages, queries, responses, etc. The use of HTML pages on the Internet has provided a ready tool for creation and use of documents in a groupware system. Security of information may dictate that access is limited to authorized personnel and that management of documents is tightly regulated.

GSM (Global System for Mobile communications)
Cellular phone technology that is predominant in

guest

Europe, but is also used around the world. GSM phones use a SIM CARD that contains user account information. The phone is programmed by inserting the card, so GSM phones can be easily rented or borrowed. GSM provides a SHORT MESSAGING SERVICE for TEXT MESSAGING.

guest

An access privilege in a LOCAL AREA NETWORK that allows an infrequent user to examine certain files on the network without having a PASSWORD.

guest book

A form that visitors to a WEBSITE are asked to complete, giving basic information, such as name, EMAIL address, and phone number. Often they are legitimate, allowing someone to measure the success of their site, for example. However, guest books are also used to compile mailing lists that are then sold to other companies. They are a prime source of SPAM.

GUI

see GRAPHICAL USER INTERFACE.

gutter

An additional margin added to a word processing document or page layout document that allows space for a binder without obscuring the text.

H

hacker
The term usually refers to someone who accesses other people's computers, with the aid of communications technology, and without permission.

half height drive
A DISK DRIVE that occupies approximately 1.6 inches height in a computer drive bay. Originally the drive bay was 31/2 inches high to accommodate the original size of a disk drive. Disk drives have shrunk in size since those early days.

halftone
The shading in an image created by use of dots of various sizes and densities. Light areas are represented by small dots spaced apart while dark areas are created by larger dots placed close together. A similar technique can be used to produce flowing colors. Images scanned into a computer can be created in halftones to create usable images for reproduction.

hand-held scanner
A scanning device (*see* SCANNER) that can be held in the hand. The scanning head is moved over the text or image to be copied. The image or text is digitized and can be stored in the computer. The image is held as a bit-mapped file (*see* BITMAP) and as such any text in it cannot be edited. However, OPTICAL CHARACTER RECOGNITION software can be used to translate the text into a usable file that can be manipulated like any text file.

handhelds

handhelds
A DEVICE that can be easily held in the hands and operated. Generally, it refers to PDAs, but it could also refer to any EMBEDDED DEVICE that you can hold and use, e.g. a DIGITAL CAMERA.

handle
A small black square that surrounds a GRAPHICS image in an OBJECT ORIENTED PROGRAM, allowing the user to change the size of the image or to reshape the image or to move the image around the screen. By choosing the appropriate handle, the image can be changed in one or two dimensions.

handshaking
A greeting between two devices, such as a modem to modem or computer to printer, that signals that data transmission between the devices can proceed. The two types are *hardware handshaking* and *software handshaking*. In hardware handshaking a control wire is used to signal when transmission can proceed. In software handshaking, such as XON/XOFF, a control code is sent to control the flow of data.

hanging indent
In a word processing program this is the format of a paragraph that has the first line starting on the left margin and the subsequent lines starting further to the right, as in this text.

hard
A term used to describe a hyphen or PAGE BREAK inserted by the user in a word processing, page layout or spread-

sheet program, as opposed to a SOFT command inserted by the program.

hard card
A printed CIRCUIT BOARD (PCB) that plugs into the EXPANSION SLOT of a computer. The PCB contains a hard disk drive and controller circuitry. This is an easy way of adding extra storage capacity to a computer but it is an expensive option.

hard copy
A document or file that is printed as opposed to one that is stored in a computer's memory or stored on disk.

hard disk
A fixed disk that forms a storage medium within the computer. It was developed in 1973 by IBM and initially called the Winchester disk, but early versions were very expensive. Today they are a standard component of just about every computer and their mass production has reduced the price enormously. At the same time, the capacity has risen dramatically, from the early sizes of 10, 20 and 40 MEGABYTES to multiple GIGABYTES. The hard disk includes the storage medium, the READ/WRITE HEAD and the electronics to connect it to the computer. There are several disks, or platters, that revolve at 3600 rpm, and the head floats just above the disk surface to eliminate wear.

hardware
All of the equipment that comprises the physical aspects of a SYSTEM, e.g. monitor, keyboard, etc., down to the detail of cables and chips.

hardware interrupt

hardware interrupt
see INTERRUPT.

hardware platform
The physical equipment of a computer system such as the CENTRAL PROCESSING UNIT, DISK DRIVE(s), VDU and PRINTER. In fact, anything that can be connected to a computer.

Hayes command set
A standard set of instructions that have been developed to control communications through MODEMs. Commands include:

AT	attention command prefix
Hn	hang up
A	answer
Ln	speaker volume
D	dial
P	pulse dialing
Fn	select line modulation

Hayes compatible modem
A MODEM that recognizes the HAYES COMMAND SET, which is the *de facto* standard for ASYNCHRONOUS COMMUNICATIONS between modems.

HDLC (High-level Data Link Control)
A PROTOCOL for synchronous communications.

head
The device used by a DISK DRIVE to read a disk. As each side of a disk can be read by a separate head the number of heads is often used as shorthand for the number of sides (e.g. double-sided disk).

Hertz (Hz)

head crash
The physical impact of a disk head on the disk, resulting in damage to its surface and a serious equipment malfunction that usually destroys data stored on the disk. It was relatively common on older systems, but modern high-tolerance engineering ensures that head crashes rarely occur.

header
Text that is placed at the top of every page in a document. The header normally contains the date, page number and document title. Different word processing programs have a variety of controls over the headers in a document.

heap
A part of the computer's memory that is set aside for specific instructions that control such aspects as user input, menus and icons.

help
A file built into a software program that provides assistance and further information about selected topics. The file can be opened while the program continues to run.

Hertz (Hz)
A measure of the frequency at which electrical waves repeat each second. It is a measurement used to show the speed of a computer CHIP. Generally, the higher the speed of a chip the better is the performance. However, two different chips can operate at the same speed but have different performance levels. A computer with a fast PROCESSOR is not necessarily ideal since it depends

on the quality of DATA BUS, display (*see* VDU) and DISK DRIVES to determine the performance of a system.

heuristic
A method used by experts to solve problems using a rule of thumb rather than strict logic. This is important in developing ARTIFICIAL INTELLIGENCE and knowledge systems.

hexadecimal
A numbering system that uses a base of 16 using characters 0-9 and A-F to represent 0-15.

Decimal	*Hexadecimal*	*Binary*
0	0	0000
1	1	0001
2	2	0010
3	3	0011
4	4	0100
5	5	0101
6	6	0110
7	7	0111
8	8	1000
9	9	1001
10	A	1010
11	B	1011
12	C	1100
13	D	1101
14	E	1110
15	F	1111
16	10	10000

HFS (Hierarchical File System)
A disk storage system developed by APPLE to organize

files on a HARD DISK. The system allows storage of files in a series of FOLDERS. A folder can be stored in a folder within a folder, etc.

hidden code
An invisible code or instruction in a document that controls the appearance of the document when printed. Different codes control styles such as bold type or paragraph indents.

hidden file
A file that is rendered invisible because of the way its file attributes have been set. The file cannot be seen in directory listings because it is judged so important that the file should not be altered or deleted.

hierarchy
Structure that has a predetermined ordering from high to low; an ordering of OBJECTS. All files and folders on the HARD DISK are organized in a hierarchy. *See also* TREE STRUCTURE.

high density
A storage technique for FLOPPY DISKS that store over 1.44 or 2 megabytes of data on the disk. The disk media must use relatively expensive fine-grained magnetic particles to be capable of storage in high density format.

high resolution
The extra sharpness of the RESOLUTION of high quality PRINTERS and VDUs that produces output with smooth curves and well-defined fonts with no jagged edges. The resolution of a printer or screen is measured in

high-level programming language

DOTS PER INCH or in the number of PIXELs that can be displayed.

high-level programming language

A set of commands for computers that people can understand. Once the programmer has completed the program, all the commands in the high-level programming language are compiled into their equivalent machine code. The use of high-level languages such as BASIC, C or PASCAL allows the programmer to concentrate on solving the problem rather than on how to tell the computer to perform calculations.

highlight

To select an area of a document in order to apply a command to that area or otherwise work with the selection. The selected area is often displayed in REVERSE VIDEO. It is most commonly defined using the mouse by clicking and holding until the desired area is selected.

history

The history on a web browser is a listing of all recently-visited sites on the Internet. Although it is comparatively easy to move backwards or forwards to sites seen over the last 30 minutes of browsing, this does eventually fall down. Scrolling down the history file provides a list of recently visited sites, which can be revisited by selecting the appropriate address.

hit

The retrieval of an item from a WEB SERVER. Calling up a WEB PAGE equals one hit. Hit counts, therefore, are a good measure of site TRAFFIC.

Also, any time some data matches some criteria, e.g. the results from a SEARCH ENGINE.

HMA (High Memory Area)
An area of 64 KILOBYTES of memory in a DOS system above the first MEGABYTE of memory.

holographic storage
A storage technology that uses three-dimensional images created by light patterns projected and stored on photosensitive material. When it becomes available it will store a greater amount of information than CD ROMs.

home computer
A computer that is designed or marketed for home use as opposed to office or work use. It is generally perceived as being of lower power or capability than a business computer. However, this distinction is becoming less obvious as the technology advances.

home key
A key on a keyboard that has various uses depending on the program being utilized. Normally the home key will move the cursor to the beginning of the current line, current paragraph or current document.

home page
The opening page of a WEBSITE, where the title and contents of the website are introduced. BROWSERS allow for you to set a personal home page that may simply be a FAVORITE, and many websites provide a page that you can customize and adopt as such a personal home page.

host

This will always be the page that first opens when you launch your browser.

host

A COMPUTER that acts as a source of information. The term can refer to almost any kind of computer, from a mainframe that is a host to its terminals, to a SERVER that is host to its CLIENTS, to a desktop computer that is host to its PERIPHERALS.

hot key

A keyboard key combination shortcut that gives access to a menu command or direct access to a program.

hot link

A connection between two distinct documents that automatically copies information from one document (the source) to the other document (the target). Changing the information in the source document will result in a similar change in the target document. *See* HYPERLINK; LINK.

hot spot

In an HTML document, an area of an OBJECT (e.g. an image file), or some text, that activates a FUNCTION when selected, e.g. open another WEB PAGE, or an image or video file, or carry out some other action. The function is launched via a HYPERLINK, so the TARGET must be a valid file. *See also* IMAGE MAP; WEB DESIGN.

Also, in general, a point in an APPLICATION or SYSTEM or NETWORK where activity is at its greatest. *See* CHOKEPOINT.

hot swapping

To be able to add and remove external devices while a

computer is running, and have the OPERATING SYSTEM automatically recognize and deal with the change. This is a feature of USB. *See also* PLUG AND PLAY.

hotspot
A geographic location where a WIRELESS NETWORK transceiver allows a subscriber to have access to network services, particularly the Internet, via a LAPTOP or mobile phone, for instance. Hotspots are usually located in highly public places e.g. mass transit termini, such as airports, railroad stations, libraries, convention centers and hotels. Hotspots have a very short range. *See* ACCESS POINT; MOBILE INTERNET; WAP.

housekeeping
Activities that are performed to reduce clutter on the computer desktop and disks and generally make for efficient use of the computer. Housekeeping includes deleting unwanted files and programs, reorganizing files into the most appropriate directories, decrementing disks (*see* FRAGMENTATION), etc.

HTML (Hypertext Markup Language)
The basic language in which pages on the web are written. The use of HTML enables links to be employed which means that an interconnection can be generated between parts of a site, documents, words and documents, etc. Such links are commonly shown in a different color (and also underlined) and when a link has been utilized, the color changes.

HTML consists of the text required, to which must be added certain formatting codes which are called tags. Also, if a photograph or graphic is to be included,

HTML document

instructions have to be created for its placement. Many of the web creation packages have wizards to make the process easier. The tags involve a description of the style required between the signs < >. Thus to put something in italics would require:

<ITALIC> Welcome </ITALIC>

One of the basic properties of HTML is that it facilitates the use of links.

HTML document

A DOCUMENT file composed of HTML. Often synonymous with WEB PAGE, but it is worthwhile remembering that not all HTML documents are used as web pages, e.g. MULTIMEDIA presentations. *See* WEB AUTHORING.

HTML editor

A simple HTML document authoring TOOL that is basically a text editor that has been adopted for writing HTML CODE. It can carry out most functions associated with straightforward coding, but does involve having to work with the code itself. Historically, it has always been recommended that newcomers to the field learn this type of authoring initially. *See also* WEB AUTHORING.

HTTP (Hyper Text Transport Protocol)

The abbreviation http precedes the address of a website, in the form http://www. And so on. HTTP is the structure used to connect the many servers on the web and it allows pages in HTML format to be sent to the computer being used for browsing. It is commonly the case that the http is not necessary when typing in an address, but it will be shown on the address line at the top of the screen.

hypertext

hub
A device at the center of a computing system to which all the computers in a network are connected, allowing intercommunication.

hybrid disk
see DUAL-PLATFORM DISK.

HyperCard
An accessory program authored by APPLE. Originally this program was shipped with every Macintosh but it is now supplied commercially.

hyperlink
A link set-up between objects. The link can be text, as icon, or graphic. Pages on the web commonly have links which may connect with other pages on that site, another site completely or may enable an email to be sent.

hypermedia
A term used to describe how hypertext concepts can be applied to multimedia.

hypertalk
A computer scripting language that is used to create instructions for HYPERCARD programs. Hypertalk is an event-oriented language (*see* EVENT-DRIVEN PROGRAM).

hypertext
The ability to pick up on one word in a document as a route to another area of a document. For example, in a hypertext dictionary a link would exist between a headword and the same word when used in a definition.

Hz

By clicking on "document" in this definition the computer would be directed to the definition of "document". Such a system is used in the worldwide web to connect pages of related information.

Hz
see HERTZ.

I

I/O
see INPUT/OUPUT.

IAP
see INTERNET ACCESS PROVIDER.

IBM personal computer (IBM PC)
A PERSONAL COMPUTER developed by IBM that was released in 1981.

icon
A symbol on screen that represents something or some process or function in the computer. Icons are used in a GRAPHICAL USER INTERFACE, and the image of an icon resembles the result of choosing that particular option or command. Programs resident within WINDOWS use numerous icons for tasks such as opening and closing files (which use small pictures of files), printing (a printer), discarding files (a trash can), and so on. Icons can also represent software programs and enable rapid access to the appropriate program.

IDE interface
A type of disk controller that is built into the hard disk drive, cutting out the need for a separate controller or ADAPTER CARD. The drive that connects directly to the MOTHERBOARD is relatively fast and inexpensive.

idle time
The time during which the computer is turned on but

if

is not processing any instructions. The computer is waiting for a COMMAND.

if

A LOGICAL OPERATOR that tests a CONDITIONAL STATEMENT and, if it is true, performs one task; if it is false, it performs another task.

illegal character
A character that is not recognized by a command-driven operating system (*see* EVENT-DRIVEN PROGRAM) in a particular situation. For example, in DOS you cannot use an asterisk (*) or a space when naming a file.

IM
see INSTANT MESSAGING.

image editor
A PAINT PROGRAM that contains many more features, including the ability to work with OBJECT ORIENTED GRAPHICS. These applications also support other features of DRAW PROGRAMS. Each OBJECT, however, is represented as a BITMAP, as in paint programs.

Image editors place each object in an image in a different LAYER, thus simulating independence. An application that allows you to edit photographs, e.g. Adobe Photoshop, is an example of an image editor.

image enhancement
The improvement of a GRAPHICS image by smoothing out the jagged edges, changing the colors, adjusting the contrast or removing unwanted details.

imaging

image map
Often spelt as one word, an image map (or imagemap) is a WEB PAGE graphic image that contains at least one HYPERLINK to other web pages or application files, e.g. a page that displays a geographical map of branch locations, where the branch areas of the map link to pages giving individual information about that branch. These days, WEB AUTHORING software provides comprehensive TOOLS for creating image maps.
Essentially, an image map is an HTML LAYER, laid over the top of an ordinary image file. The individual hyperlink areas of the image are known as HOT SPOTs. Image maps are used extensively on the WORLDWIDE WEB.
See also NAVIGATION BAR; WEB DESIGN.

image processing
Any process that relates to manipulation of images from the initial digitizing to manipulating the image (embellishing and refining), saving the image and printing the image.

image setter
A high quality, professional grade typesetting machine that creates images at RESOLUTIONS of 1200 DOTS PER INCH or more.

imaging
Creating a RASTER image of any CONTINUOUS TONE image, by *scanning* or *screening* the image to turn it into a matrix of dots (a BITMAP), allowing it to be processed by a computer or other system and displayed or printed. This could refer to a photograph or some text, or the taking of a digital photograph. *See also* COLOR REPRODUCTION; DIGITAL CAMERA.

impact printer

impact printer
A printer that relies on contact with the paper and an ink ribbon to imprint the character. It is noisy but has the advantage of being able to produce multiple copies of documents

import
To open a file that has been created in one application in another application. The file must be in a form that the new application can read it or the new application must have conversion codes available to it.

incremental backup
A backup procedure that takes a copy of only the files on a disk that have been updated since the previous backup was taken. FULL BACKUP takes a copy of all files irrespective of when they were last backed up.

index
A list of key words created at the end of a document. The index contains the word and the page references where that word can be found. Some word processing and desktop publishing programs create indexes automatically.

index file
A file in a DATABASE MANAGEMENT PROGRAM that keeps a list of the location of records using a pointer system. This allows the sorting and searching of a database to be much faster if the whole record is used.

infection
Having a VIRUS in a computer system. The virus may not be immediately obvious as it can be present on a

system for many months before it is activated. This can be caused by a particular series of keystrokes or it may happen on a special date. The activated virus may cause severe problems, or simply display a rude message.

information
DATA that has been compiled into a meaningful form. Information is often used interchangeably with data but this is incorrect.

information superhighway
The global network of computers connected by satellites and telephone lines. (*See also* INTERNET).

information technology (IT)
A jargon term used to describe all computer, telecommunications and related technology that is concerned with the handling or transfer of information. IT is a vast field incorporating the collection, handling, storage and communication of INFORMATION.

init
In the Macintosh operating system a UTILITY file that is executed at start-up. It is similar to "terminate" and "stay" resident programs in the DOS operating environment. Inits can conflict with each other and cause a system CRASH. Inits include disk drive drivers, fax card drivers, etc.

initialize
To start up or set up the basic conditions. (*See also* FORMAT.)

inkjet printer

inkjet printer
A printer type that forms an image by spraying ink on to a page from a matrix of tiny spray jets.

input
The INFORMATION to be entered into a computer system for subsequent processing.

input device
Any peripheral device that provides a means of getting data into the computer. The term thus includes the keyboard, mouse, modem, scanner, graphics tablet.

input/output (I/O)
The general term for the equipment and system that is used to communicate with a computer. It ensures that program instructions and data readily go into and come out of the CENTRAL PROCESSING UNIT.

insert mode
The input mode that allows input to be typed into a document at the CURSOR point. Text already in the document will be moved to allow for the new entries. Overtype mode, on the other hand, deletes previous type as new material is inserted.

insertion point
The point at which text can be entered into a document when typing. It is analogous to the CURSOR in old DOS systems.

installation program
A UTILITY PROGRAM that is commonly supplied with application software with the purpose of assisting the

Integrated Services Digital Network

user in installing the software correctly on a hard disk. The utility ensures that the correct system files are located on the hard disk and ensures that the various files are located in the correct DIRECTORY or FOLDER.

instant messaging (IM)
Exchanging messages in REAL TIME between two or more people. The technology that enables CHAT to take place. When the user logs in, they will be informed who else is ONLINE. They also receive any messages and everyone else is informed that they are now online. They can then interact. In a business environment, IM can be a rapid and very effective way of communicating within a workgroup, or more distantly.

integrated circuit
A module of electronic circuitry that consists of transistors and other electronic components, usually contained on a rigid board. A variety of boards are plugged into a computer to enable it to perform its various tasks.

integrated program
A group of software packages each with a logical relationship to the other components. For example, a typical integrated package may include a word processor, a spreadsheet, a database, a graphics application and perhaps a communications application. The common link is that all these applications operate in a similar manner and it is possible to transfer data between them.

Integrated Services Digital Network
see ISDN.

integrity

integrity
The quality associated with a file that is complete and uncorrupted. For various reasons a file can be corrupted. In this case the file is said to have "lost its integrity."

Intel
A major manufacturing company that makes integrated chips. The range of chips started with the popular 80286 processor and has progressed to the Pentium and new generations of chip.

interactive processing
A system in which the user can monitor the computer's processing directly on the computer screen and make any corrections to the process that are required. In the early days of computers, processing relied on BATCH PROCESSING, when the user had to wait hours to obtain the results of the program.

interface
The term for the PORTS and the correct electronic CONFIGURATION between two or more devices. (*See also* USER INTERFACE.)

interlaced
A VDU display technology that produces HIGH RESOLUTION pictures but rapidly moving pictures may appear to flicker or streak. Only half the screen is refreshed (*see* REFRESH) on the first pass with the second half of the screen refreshed on the second pass.

internal command
A DOS command that is always available at the DOS

PROMPT. The COMMAND.COM program is loaded on startup and contains codes for common internal commands such as copy, dir, prompt and CD (change directory). External commands run separate program files.

internal hard disk
A HARD DISK that is located inside the PERSONAL COMPUTER's case. It uses the main computer's power supply and is consequently cheaper than an external hard drive.

internal memory
Another name given to RAM and ROM, which is where the computer stores information being used by a program or file.

internal modem
A modem that resides inside the case of a personal computer and connects via an expansion slot.

Internet
A worldwide system of linked computer networks. The system can link computers that have different operating systems and storage techniques. The first commercial account occurred in 1990 and since then it has been known as the Internet. It all began in the late 1950s in the USA with the Advanced Research Projects Agency (ARPA). Some years later, ARPA created an embryonic net for military research networking. Later, universities and other organizations became involved and in the early 1970s the network crossed the Atlantic. Parallel developments in computer hardware and software brought electronic mail and file transfer protocol and ultimately the domain name system. Arpanet was the first working net that could be demonstrated to use

Internet access

the new network technology and necessary protocols. The Internet developed from Arpanet and the idea was to have many separate networks joined later by more ground and satellite networks. The fundamental building block was developed by Kleinrock and involved data transmission by packet switching (sending data in separate parts rather than in one line along a circuit) and the facility for computers to talk together. Then open architecture networking allowed different networks to link and work together and this underlies the vast Internet of today.

A formal definition of the Internet has been coined by the Federal Networking Council as follows:

"Internet; refers to the global information system that
(i) is logically linked together by a globally unique address space based on the Internet Protocol (IP) or its subsequent extensions/follow-ons;
(ii) is able to support communications using the transmission control protocol/Internet protocol (TCP/IP) suite or its subsequent extensions/follow-ons, and/or other IP-compatible protocols; and
(iii) provides, uses or makes accessible, either publicly or privately, high level services layered on the communications and related infrastructure described herein."

Inevitably there have been many changes in the Internet, notably the worldwide web and email and the changes will inevitably continue.

Internet access

There are many companies offering online services as Internet service providers. Some have packages for both business and the home user and all that is required is an appropriate computer with modem, a phone line and

Internet publishing

software from the provider in question. (*See also* INTERNET ACCESS PROVIDER; INTERNET SERVICE PROVIDER).

Internet access provider (IAP)
Originally synonymous with ISP. Now, companies that sell high-speed Internet access to ISPs and other organizations and companies.

Internet address
see ADDRESS.

Internet café
see CYBER CAFÉ.

Internet domain name
see DOMAIN NAME.

Internet Explorer
The internationally known BROWSER from MICROSOFT. Versions for Windows, Macintosh and Unix are available. Internet Explorer was developed after NETSCAPE launched its Navigator browser, and the companies ended up in a head-to-head competition. Despite litigation, it could be said that Microsoft won, for Internet Explorer has become the market leader.

Internet publishing
remembering that the INTERNET is the physical global NETWORK, while the WORLDWIDE WEB is part of the content of that network, Internet publishing does not just refer to the creation of a WEBSITE. Essentially, it means making any electronic DOCUMENT available on the Internet, from PROGRAM files to PDFs. Many writers and artists, and not a few

publishers, are finding the Internet to be an invaluable way of "getting out there". There is, after all, a global audience.

Internet relay chat (IRC)
see CHAT.

Internet service provider (ISP)
A company that allows people to connect up to the Internet through their own computer system. Major service providers, such as AOL, offer a wide range of additional services (*see also* ONLINE SERVICE).

interpreter
A routine that translates a program written in a HIGH-LEVEL PROGRAMMING LANGUAGE into MACHINE LANGUAGE. The interpreter translates each command one at a time and then, once the computer has executed the command, it moves to the next line. If an error has been made in the program the interpreter stops and reports an ERROR MESSAGE. (*See also* COMPILER.)

interrupt
A signal from the microprocessor that temporarily halts or interrupts processing to allow another operation such as receipt of input to take place. As soon as the operation has been completed the original process continues. The computer is constantly faced with such situations. These are called *hardware interrupts* as opposed to *software interrupts,* which are interrupt signals generated by a computer program.

interrupt request
see IRQ.

intranet
A NETWORK that works in a similar way to the INTERNET, but which has limited access and is not generally available to the public. Intranets are generally operated by businesses and institutions, as a way of sharing and communicating information around the organization. There is usually also an ACCESS POINT to the Internet.

IP
See TCP/IP.

IP address
A unique ADDRESS which identifies a computer and the NETWORK in which it resides by a series of four numbers separated by full stops. The address is used by the TCP/IP PROTOCOLS to send data to the destination computer, which will then respond. This is basically how the Internet works.

IRC (Internet Relay Chat)
see CHAT.

IRQ (Interrupt ReQuest)
A "line" used to signal the CPU that a PERIPHERAL is starting or finishing a task. Prior to the advent of PCI, two devices could not use the same line, consequently changes to a system's peripherals often required the physical configuration of the IRQs, via a DIP SWITCH on the MOTHERBOARD. An IRQ CONFLICT used to be a common BUG. *See also* INTERRUPT; PCI; PLUG AND PLAY.

ISA (Industry Standard Architecture)
A common PC EXPANSION BUS, it accepts PLUG-IN boards

ISDN (Integrated Services Digital Network)

for audio, video and other PERIPHERALS. Most PCs today have a combination of ISA and PCI slots, but ISA is expected to become obsolete very soon.

ISDN (Integrated Services Digital Network)

A means of transmitting data, voice and video, digitally over a telecommunications line. The special line is quieter than conventional lines both in transmission and connection, and it has several channels which provide greater flexibility and capacity. Internet access can be made using an ISDN line but a terminal adapter is necessary with the matching software.

ISO 9660

A DATA format designed by the International Standards Organization, which is a cross-platform PROTOCOL for FILE and DIRECTORY names. File names are restricted to UPPERCASE letters, the digits 0 to 9 and the underscore character. Directory names can be up to eight characters (with no extension) with a maximum of eight subdirectories. Most Macintosh computers could recognize these names. *See also* DUAL-PLATFORM DISK; CD BURNING.

ISP

see INTERNET SERVICE PROVIDER.

IT

see INFORMATION TECHNOLOGY.

iteration

A COMMAND or program statement that is continually repeated until a particular condition is met. A simple iteration is: add one to a number until the number is equal to 10.

J

jaggies or aliasing
The ragged edges that appear on computer GRAPHICS. They are caused by the square edges of PIXELS, which show up when a curve is drawn.

Java
A programming language developed by Sun Microsystems. It is designed to be usable on any computer system so a program can be written in Java and someone else with Java can use it, irrespective of the computer type – true cross-platform compatibility. In practice, it is slightly different, but Java was picked up very quickly by web users because it gave more scope and the ability to create animation-like features using JavaScript. Whereas Java is a separate entity, JavaScript uses HTML and can be used by a web browser. The former has to download and run an applet. Recent versions of some browsers have Java interpreters included to remove the need for extra software.

JavaScript
Created by Netscape, this uses HTML as the interface and it resides within the web page. It allows a variety of website features to be created (for example, a clock) and there are numerous sites providing information on JavaScript and its uses.

jewel case
The hard plastic, hinged box-like container that is used

job
to package a CD. Also known as a jewel box.

job
An item of work that is performed by a computer, such as BACKGROUND printing of documents.

job queue
A series of jobs that a computer is to perform in sequence.

join
In a RELATIONAL DATABASE, information from two separate data tables is combined or joined to create another data table that contains summary information.

Joliet
A DATA format produced by Microsoft that allowed for much longer FILE and DIRECTORY names and structure than in ISO 9660. A "reader" was subsequently produced for Macintoshes – an important step that stopped file name corruption in CROSS-PLATFORM operations. *See also* DUAL-PLATFORM DISK; CD BURNING.

joystick
An INPUT DEVICE controlling the cursor of a computer. The joystick is normally used for controlling computer games.

JPEG (Joint Photographic Experts Group)
A FILE COMPRESSION technique which enables image file sizes to be reduced by as much as 96 per cent, with negligible loss of detail. The technique uses "lossy compression," which deliberately dumps some data, but

in images with several million colors the effect is often not noticed.

JSP (Java Server Page)
An extension to JAVA technology that provides a simple programming vehicle for displaying DYNAMIC CONTENT on a web page. JSP is an HTML page with embedded Java source CODE that is executed in the WEB SERVER. The HTML provides the page layout that will be returned to the web BROWSER, and Java provides the processing.

junk email
see SPAM.

justification
The alignment of lines of text in a paragraph along the margins. Text can be aligned with the left margin, right margin or both.

K

K
The abbreviation for kilo as in kilometers. It actually means 1000, but in the computer world it is used rather more loosely because 1 KILOBYTE is actually 1024 bytes. It is commonly used to refer to the relative size of a computer's main memory. 64K is equal to approximately 64,000 characters of information.

Kb, Kbytes
see KILOBYTE.

Kermit
An ASYNCHRONOUS COMMUNICATIONS protocol that is used for telephone communications.

kern
To reduce or increase the space between two characters in a display font with the result of placing the characters in a pleasing style.

kernel
The part of the OPERATING SYSTEM that loads first. Because it stays in main memory, it is important that it is as small as possible while still providing all the services required of it. The kernel is responsible for memory, process, task, and disk management.

key
A button on a keyboard.

key field
The FIELD that is used as the one for sorting data. For example, a SORT of records in a database of customers using the second name of a customer as the key field will provide an alphabetic list of customers.

keyboard
A set of alphabetic, numeric, symbol and control keys that relays the character or command to a computer, which then displays the character on the screen. The keyboard is the most frequently used INPUT DEVICE.

keypad
The same as the numeric keypad, which is the group of numbers at the right-hand side of a keyboard.

keystroke
The action of pressing a key on the keyboard resulting in a character being entered or a command being initiated.

keyword
A word in a programming language that describes an action or operation that the computer recognizes.

kilobyte (K, Kb, Kbytes)
The basic unit of measurement for computer memory equal to 1024 BYTES.

knowledge engineering
The process of extracting information from experts and expressing this knowledge in a form that an EXPERT SYSTEM can use.

L

label
Text in a SPREADSHEET program as opposed to a number or formula. A label is used for descriptive purposes such as a heading for a row or column.

LAN
see LOCAL AREA NETWORK.

landscape orientation
An optional way of printing a page of text where the page is turned on its side so that it is wider than it is long. (*See also* PORTRAIT ORIENTATION.)

language
A method of communicating. Humans use languages such as English, Spanish, French, etc, while computers use languages such as C, FORTRAN, BASIC, etc.

laptop computer
A small portable computer that can operate from its own power supply and can be used almost anywhere. It consists of an integrated LCD screen, keyboard and TRACK-BALL or TRACK-PAD. It is constructed in such a way that it can be carried and operated anywhere.

laser printer
A HIGH RESOLUTION printer that uses a technology similar to photocopiers to fuse the text or graphic images to the paper.

LDAP (Lightweight Directory Access Protocol)

LaserJet
A LASER PRINTER manufactured by Hewlett-Packard. Because of its quality and price it has come to be regarded as an industry standard.

latency
The period during which one component in a SYSTEM is waiting for another component.

In a NETWORK, the amount of time it takes a packet of DATA to travel from source to destination.

launch
To start an application or program.

layer
An on-screen sheet on which text or graphic images are placed. These images are independent from text or graphics on another sheet or layer. Such layers are used in page layout programs, graphics programs or CAD programs.

layout
The process of arranging text or graphics on a page in programs such as word processing or database management systems

LCD (Liquid Crystal Display)
A low power display system that uses crystal molecules which are excited by an electric current. LCD monitors are now becoming the standard type of DISPLAY, and are particularly useful because they are so compact.

LDAP (Lightweight Directory Access Protocol)
A PROTOCOL that is used to access a directory listing.

LED (Light Emitting Diode)

LDAP support is being implemented in browsers and email programs so that it will provide a common method for searching email addresses on the Internet. It is allied to HTTP and FTP and uses the ldap:// prefix.

LED (Light Emitting Diode)
A small light used by various computer devices to communicate information about the status of the device.

legend
The key on a GRAPH that shows the meaning of the different colors or shades.

letter quality
A style of print that matches the quality of impact printing on a typewriter. The LASER PRINTER has replaced the DAISYWHEEL PRINTER as the standard for letter quality printers.

level
in DIRECTORY STRUCTURE, an indicator of FILE location, particularly important with regard to PATHs, which step up and down levels.

Also, an expression of the complexity or state of advance of a PROGRAM or STANDARD. *See also* RELEASE; VERSION.

libraries
stores of prewritten programming routines for use in generating applications.

license
see SOFTWARE LICENCE.

light pen
A stylus used for INPUT, pointed at a computer display that is sensitive to the light from the display.

light-emitting diode
see LED.

line art
A computer drawing that consists of only black and white areas. There are no shades of gray or halftones. Thus line art can be printed on LOW RESOLUTION printers.

line feed
see FEED.

line graph
A style of graph using lines to show the relationship between the variables being plotted.

line spacing
The space between lines of text in a word processing document or page layout program. Most programs allow at least single spacing or double spacing.

link or hyperlink
The means whereby connections to other pages (on a website) or other web pages are embedded in web pages (*see* hyperlink). Also, to establish a connection between two computers (as in a network) or two programs or two files.

Linux
A freely-distributed OPERATING SYSTEM that runs on a

liquid crystal display

number of hardware platforms, including PCs and Macintoshes, Linux has become an extremely popular alternative to proprietary operating systems. Very usefully, you can simultaneously EMULATE both a Windows and a Macintosh ENVIRONMENT from within Linux.

liquid crystal display
see LCD.

LISP (LISt Processing)
A HIGH-LEVEL PROGRAMMING LANGUAGE used to a great extent in the development of ARTIFICIAL INTELLIGENCE.

list box
A box that appears as part of a DIALOG BOX and lists various options from which the user can make a choice.

Listserv
Mailing list management SOFTWARE that runs on mainframes and various Unix machines. Listserv scans EMAIL messages for the words *subscribe* and *unsubscribe*, so as to update the list.

load
To transfer a program from a computer's secondary storage to the primary memory (RAM) so that it can be activated.

local area network (LAN)
A grouping of personal computers that are linked by cables within a restricted area. This enables the users to share peripheral devices and information stored either on the individual machines or on a FILE SERVER. The flow of information around the network is controlled by

logic path

programs using PROTOCOLs or rules. ETHERNET and APPLETALK are examples of protocols.

local bus
A high speed expansion slot that allows high speed transmission of information to travel between the computer processor and a peripheral device such as a monitor. The alternative would be to use an expansion bus, which is slower.

local drive
In a network of computers the WORKSTATION might have a built-in DISK DRIVE, which is referred to as the local drive, as opposed to the server drive or remote drive.

lock
To protect a file being altered or changed either accidentally or deliberately. Files can be locked by a software utility or by physically locking a FLOPPY DISK with a WRITE/PROTECT tab.

log off
To end a session working at a computer terminal or system.

log on
To begin working at a computer terminal or system. In MS-DOS (Microsoft disk operating system) to log on means to activate a drive. In networks, a PASSWORD may be necessary to log on to the system.

logic path
In PROGRAMMING, the conceptual route followed by some DATA through the ROUTINE of a program, in order to

logical drive

achieve the goal of the program. For a logic path to work, all aspects of the logic involved must be in agreement. The process is much the same as that involved in following through a flowchart. Note that logic fits into a BINARY environment because there can only be only a "yes" or "no" result to any condition.

logical drive
see PHYSICAL DRIVE.

logical operator
A special word (e.g. AND, OR, NOT) used in a programming statement that expands or limits a search. For example, when searching a database the query may be to find all occurrences of customers living in Nashville. This could be restricted with the revised query find all customers living in Nashville AND who have purchased goods in the last month.

login
synonymous with LOG ON.

logo
A HIGH-LEVEL PROGRAMMING LANGUAGE that is commonly used in education to teach programming concepts.

look-up function
in programming, a procedure in which the program consults a pre-defined data list (*look-up table*) to obtain information or for comparison purposes.

loop
in programs and MACROS a loop is a set of instructions

that tells the computer to continue performing a task until a certain condition is met or the loop has been repeated a certain number of times.

lossy compression (see also JPEG)
An image compression technique that achieves very considerable compression and therefore much smaller files, but which on decompression does not restore the image 100% because some information is discarded in the process of compression.

low resolution
Screen or printer output that is of low quality. The fewer DOTS PER INCH that a printer can produce, the lower the quality. The fewer PIXELS on a screen the lower the quality of output. Lower resolution produces more JAGGIES on an image.

lowercase
see UPPERCASE.

low-level programming language
A style of computer language that uses codes or expressions that are similar to the MACHINE CODE instructions understood by the processor chip. (*See also* HIGH-LEVEL PROGRAMMING LANGUAGE.)

luggable
A PERSONAL COMPUTER that is too big to be described as portable but is small enough to be transported easily from place to place.

M

Mac OS
The version of the disk operating system written by APPLE that is packaged with their MACINTOSH computers.

machine code
The basic 1s and 0s a computer processor uses as its instructions.

machine language
A BINARY language that all computers must use. Machine code uses the lowest form of coding, binary, to instruct the machine to change the numbers in memory locations. All other computer languages must be compiled from their high-level code into machine code before the programs can be executed.

Macintosh
A line of computers designed and manufactured by Apple Computer. First released in 1984, they introduced GRAPHICAL USER INTERFACE to the PERSONAL COMPUTER world.

macro
A record of commands used regularly in an application that can be activated by a keystroke. The macro could be a list of commands used to print a report. Without the macro, the report will require several commands to be executed while if they are recorded in a macro, one command or keystroke can be initiated to print the report.

magnetic disk
A secondary storage device that consists of a plastic disk coated with magnetically sensitive material. Magnetic disks are usually described as floppy disks or hard disks depending on their construction. Hard disks generally have a higher storage capacity.

magnetic field
A force surrounding electrical devices that can have an adverse effect on data stored on MAGNETIC MEDIA.

magnetic media
Any of a wide variety of disks or tapes, coated or impregnated with magnetic material, on which information can be recorded and stored. The magnetic coating is repositioned when influenced by a MAGNETIC FIELD, and the READ/WRITE HEAD emits a magnetic field when writing to the disk or tape, which produces a positive or negative charge corresponding to that item of data. When reading, the head senses the charges and decodes them. Disks are used universally but for very high capacity storage, magnetic TAPE is ideal.

magnetic tape
see TAPE.

mail gateway
An electronic path that allows ELECTRONIC MAIL to be sent between different mail services or direct to a computer on the INTERNET.

mail merge
The process of merging two files for the purpose of

mailbox

creating a mail shot. One file consists of a letter while the second file consists of a database of names and addresses. Each name and address in the database is merged with the letter, creating a letter addressed to each name in the database.

mailbox

Within the ELECTRONIC MAIL system, a disk file or memory area in which messages for a particular destination (or person) are placed. Modern BULLETIN BOARD communications systems use a mailbox metaphor to store messages for electronic mail users. The bulletin board system is a telecommunications utility that facilitates informal communication between computer users.

main memory
see RAM.

mainframe

Any large computer such as an IBM or a Cray. They do not use the same architecture as small desktop computers and are intended for use by many people, usually within a large organization. To begin with, it referred to the large cabinet that held the CENTRAL PROCESSING UNIT and then to the large computers, developed in the 1960s, that could accommodate hundreds of DUMB TERMINALS. Now the word mainframe applies to a computing system that serves the needs of a whole organization.

margin

The space between the edge of a page and the start of the text.

markup language

A text-processing LANGUAGE where commands are embedded into the text. These instruct a DISPLAY device or printer to carry out formatting. The commands are present in a set of labels, known as TAGS, which indicate where FONT and other FORMAT elements start and stop. The text document is thus turned into the equivalent of a database RECORD.

Markup languages were originally the standard medium for word and document processing. SGML came first and served as the foundation for HTML and XML – the languages of the WORLDWIDE WEB. *See also* EMBEDDING; RENDER; WEB DESIGN.

mask

in databases, a FILTER that includes or excludes certain values.

In GRAPHICS image editing, to add a LAYER that covers over an area of the image, in order to select it for some further operation. *See also* CLIPPING PATH.

math coprocessor

A chip used for performing FLOATING POINT CALCULATIONS.

Mb, mbyte

see MEGABYTE.

media player

SOFTWARE that plays audio, video or animation files. These applications usually come with a sophisticated FRONT END CONSOLE. Well-known examples are RealPlayer, QuickTime and Windows Media Player. *See also* SKIN.

megabyte (Mb, mbyte)

megabyte (Mb, mbyte)
One million bytes (characters) of information. The common storage measurement for memory and hard disks, e.g. 4 megabytes of RAM, with a 210-megabyte HARD DISK drive.

megahertz (MHz)
A measurement of one million hertz, i.e. cycles per second. This is the unit used for computers and refers to the speed of the central processing unit. Current speeds tend to be 366 MHz, 400 MHz, 466 MHz, 550 MHz or 700 MHz. The higher speeds mean the computer operates more quickly, but 700 MHz does not necessarily mean almost twice the speed of a 366 MHz processor because processing depends upon several factors, including disk speed, software and cache size.

membrane keyboard
A style of keyboard covered by a touch sensitive material to prevent liquid or dirt entering the keyboard circuits.

memory
The circuitry and devices that are capable of storing data as well as programs. Memory is the computer's primary storage area, e.g. RAM as distinguished from the SECONDARY STORAGE of disks. Typical memory devices are SIMMs, which are plugged into the MOTHERBOARD of the computer. SIMMs are plug-in modules that contain all the necessary chips to add more RAM to a computer. The motherboard is the large circuit board that contains the CENTRAL PROCESSING UNIT, RAM, EXPANSION SLOTS and other microprocessors.

memory address
A code or name that refers to a specific location where data is stored in a computer's RAM.

memory cache
see CACHE.

memory card
A removable DEVICE used for storing data in HANDHELDS, particularly with reference to DIGITAL CAMERAS. They consist of FLASH MEMORY in various formats, such as Compact Flash and SmartMedia.

memory management
The process of efficiently using a computer's memory. Most OPERATING SYSTEMS have built-in memory management systems to control the use of memory and its allocation between conflicting programs.

memory map
Shows how the OPERATING SYSTEM utilizes the RAM.

memory resident program
A program that remains in memory ready for use at any time. The program occupies a proportion of the RAM.

memory stick
A type of MEMORY CARD originally devised by Sony that utilizes a USB connection and a commonly recognized format. Sticks of up to 1Gb are now available and are a very popular way of easily transporting and exchanging data between computers and HANDHELDS, regardless of PLATFORM. *See also* FLASH MEMORY.

menu

menu
A list of commands, applications, or other options that are available to the computer user on a monitor or VDU. A PULL DOWN MENU is a selection of commands that appears after a command on the MENU BAR of a program has been selected. A command or action is selected and often another menu will appear. Menu-driven software contains programs that proceed to the next step only when the user responds to a menu prompt.

menu bar
The area of a screen that is given over to the listing of menu items.

menu-driven program
A program that proceeds to the next step only when the user responds to a menu prompt.

merge
To draw two pieces of information or records together to create a new file or for a particular purpose, such as merging a letter file in a word processor with a data record in a database to create a mailshot.

microchip
see CHIP; MICROPROCESSOR.

microcomputer
A term sometimes used to describe a small computer system. Initially it referred to any computer that had certain key units on one INTEGRATED CIRCUIT, called the MICROPROCESSOR. The first PERSONAL COMPUTERS, designed for single users, were called microcomputers

because their CENTRAL PROCESSING UNITS were microprocessors.

microfloppy
A 3 1/2 inch FLOPPY DISK. It is encased in a plastic shell to protect it from superficial damage.

microprocessor or microchip
An electronic device (INTEGRATED CIRCUIT) that has been programmed to follow a set of logic-driven rules. It is essentially the heart of any computer system. Also, a processor that is contained on one chip.

microsecond (μs)
one millionth of a second.

Microsoft
The largest independent software company in the world. It was founded by Paul Allen and Bill Gates in 1975 and began producing programming languages such as MBASIC. Microsoft's major breakthrough came when it produced DOS and Windows for PCs. MSDOS (Microsoft disk operating system) is an almost ubiquitous program, appearing on almost every new PC along with the current version of Windows. There are many other Microsoft programs covering word processing (Word), spreadsheets (Excel), Internet (Internet Explorer) etc.

Microsoft Office
Microsoft's almost universal desktop applications package for WINDOWS and MACINTOSH, comprising some combination of Word, Excel, PowerPoint, Access and

MIDI (Musical Instrument Digital Interface)

Outlook, along with a host of utilities, forming a complete activity package of WORD PROCESSOR, SPREADSHEET, presentation, DATABASE, and EMAIL management SOFTWARE. The applications share many common functions.

MIDI (Musical Instrument Digital Interface)

A set of standards that can be used to connect musical instruments, such as digital pianos, to computers.

migrate

To move from using one computer platform to another or from one software application to another. A user can migrate from Windows to OS/2 operating systems.

millisecond (ms)

one thousandth of a second.

MIME (multipurpose Internet mail extensions)

The commonest form in which attachments are sent with emails. MIME encodes the file for transmission and then decodes it at the receiving end.

minicomputer

A computer system, usually smaller than a mainframe but larger than a microcomputer, designed for many users.

MiniDisc

A compact DIGITAL audio DISK developed by Sony, the MiniDisc is very popular in Japan. Although it only stores 140Mb, it can hold the same amount of music as a CD, due to Sony's ATRAC compression scheme. Rewritable MiniDiscs are available in 60 and 74-minute cartridges.

MiniDisc for computer was much touted, but never took off.

mini-tower
A small tower style computer system designed to sit on a desk rather than the floor where a normal tower system would sit.

mirror site
A replica of an existing WEBSITE, used to reduce TRAFFIC and improve availability. Mirror sites are useful when the original site generates too much traffic for a single server to support. They also marginally increase the speed with which files can be accessed by users who are geographically closer to the mirror.

MIS (Management Information Systems)
The current name given to the subject of data processing.

MISC (Minimum Instruction Set Chip)
The basis of the next generation of computer chips. They take the concept of RISC chips one stage further.

MNP (Microcom Network Protocol)
A STANDARD developed by the communications company Microcom. It is primarily aimed at error detection and correction between communications devices.

mobile computing
Enabling users on the move (or at a remote location) to communicate with a NETWORK. One of the major development areas in DISTRIBUTED COMPUTING. While mobile

computing implies wireless networking, the opposite is not necessarily true, for wireless connections between fixed networks are quite common. *See* MOBILE INTERNET.

mobile Internet

Gaining access to the INTERNET using HANDHELDS, such as a PDA, or mobile phone, or by using a portable device, e.g. LAPTOP COMPUTER. *See also* WAP; WIRELESS NETWORK.

mode

The state of operation of a computer. In COMMAND mode, the computer will accept commands, in INSERT MODE, text can be inserted into an existing sentence, in EDIT mode text can be amended. A computer responds in different ways depending on the mode.

mode indicator

A message displayed on screen that indicates the MODE of operation in which the computer is set, such as EDIT mode, INSERT MODE, sleep mode, wait mode, etc).

modem (modulator/demodulator)

A device for converting a computer's DIGITAL signals into ANALOG signals that can be transmitted down a telephone line. The modem is an extremely important device, enabling communication and transfer of data all over the world. In order that modems facilitate communication between computers, the modems at each end of the line must conform to the same PROTOCOL.

module

Part of a program or set of programs capable of functioning on its own.

moiré
A type of graphic distortion seen as flickering on the screen caused by placing several high contrast line patterns too close to one another.

monitor
Another name for display, screen or VDU.

monochrome
A type of monitor that displays only black and white pixels (or black with green or another color).

monospace
A font type that uses an equal amount of space for each character in the font family:
"Courier is a monospaced font."
"Times is not a monospaced font."
The difference between a monospaced font and a proportionally spaced font can be seen in the above text.

morphing
A technique that appears to melt one image into another image to create a special effect, such as creating the impression that a person changes into a panther. The effect is created by filling in the blanks between the figures so that the change from one figure to another is gradual.

motherboard
The main printed circuit board in a computer. It contains the main processor chips, the display controllers, sound chips, etc.

Motorola

Motorola
A major manufacturer of processor chips which rival Intel's Pentium processor. The company was founded in 1928 and opened its first semiconductor plant in 1953, produced its first integrated circuits in 1960 and microprocessor in 1974. It produces microprocessors for the PowerPC range.

mouse
An input device that controls the on-screen CURSOR. Movement of the mouse on the desktop causes a similar movement of the cursor around the computer screen.

Moving Picture Experts Group
See MPEG

MP3
Short for MOVING PICTURE EXPERTS GROUP Audio Layer 3. A format for the distribution of music files over the Internet. It enables files of recorded music to be compressed to the point where it becomes feasible for an Internet user to download the music to their computer. There are a number of devices for playing music in this FORMAT, including portable players. The idea is that a collection of CDs can be replaced by MP3 files stored on a magnetic DISK DRIVE, or even on any MEMORY device, although a CD-ROM of MP3 files can only be played by a compatible player. The important point is that MP3 makes audio into DIGITAL computer files that are readily transferable and take up little memory. *See* FILE COMPRESSION.

MPEG (Moving Picture Experts Group)
A working group of the International Standards

Organization (ISO), which developed this FILE COMPRESSION method for video, of the same name. There are three versions: MPEG1 is used for Internet-based video STREAMING and MPEG2, which is used for broadcast applications. MPEG4 is a development of the two, with advanced compression technology. The file extension is MPG. *See also* MP3.

MS-DOS
Microsoft's disk operating system.

MTBF (Mean Time Between Failures)
A measure of the reliability of a computer or, more particularly, of the reliability of a component used in the manufacture of the computer.

multimedia
The process of combining computer data, sound and video images to create an environment similar to television. The market for multimedia on compact disks is now expanding rapidly.

multiplexing
A technique that is used in LOCAL AREA NETWORKS to allow several signals to pass along the cables at one time. In this way several computers can access the network simultaneously. Special multiplexing devices must be incorporated, which mix the frequency of the signals being sent along the network. The presence of these devices increases the cost of the network.

multisync monitor
A COLOR MONITOR that automatically adjusts to the input

multitasking

frequency of the adapter card that is used by the computer (VGA, super VGA, etc).

multitasking

where a computer processor can undertake more than one task or operation at a time. For example, a print job can be processed at the same time as a spreadsheet is calculating. Compare with BACKGROUND operations.

multithreading

The procedure used to describe when a program splits itself into separate tasks or threads. Each thread can operate concurrently with the others.

multi-user system

A system that allows more than one user to operate the system at any one time.

N

name
A set of characters that uniquely identifies a FILE, or other OBJECT. There are rules about naming objects, e.g. a limit on the number of characters, and which characters are allowable. Names are sometimes called *identifiers*.

Also, a newish DOMAIN NAME extension (i.e. www.mydomain.name).

nano
A prefix representing one billionth.

nanosecond (ns)
one billionth of a second. These units of measure are used to indicate the speed of operation of a computer CHIP.

nanotechnology
The study of how to make computers smaller and more efficient. The term also covers the science associated with the effect of making materials and components smaller.

native file format
The format in which a particular program saves a file. The file is saved with certain key characters or codes that tell the program about the various display options associated with the file. The native file format refers to the coding style used by the particular program. Different programs have different formats but can often use the formats for another program to assist FILE TRANSFER.

natural language

natural language
A language such as English, French, etc, as opposed to an artificial language such as BASIC or COBOL.

navigation
Traveling around a WEBSITE, or the WORLDWIDE WEB in general, by following HYPERLINKS.

Moving through the DIRECTORY STRUCTURE and menus of an APPLICATION.

Ease of navigation is one of the prime requisites of a website or application, and the ability of an individual to navigate quickly and effortlessly is both a skill and an art. *See also* ACCESSIBILITY; BREADCRUMBS; SITE MAP; WEB DESIGN.

navigation bar
A group of BUTTONS or graphic images or text used to LINK to the various sections of a WEBSITE. If the navigation bar is represented by an image that gives you various selection options, it is known as an IMAGE MAP. *See also* NAVIGATION; SITE MAP; TABLE OF CONTENTS.

near letter quality
A mode of operation for DOT MATRIX PRINTERS that produces characters at typewriter quality. This mode has become outdated because of the advent of LASER PRINTERS and INKJET PRINTERS, which produce high quality output faster and quieter.

nest
placing one OBJECT inside another object of the same type. In a text DOCUMENT, a list can be nested within another list. In WORD PROCESSING, you can nest one document inside another. In a DIRECTORY STRUCTURE, folders can be nested

Netscape

inside another. In PROGRAMMING, a loop operation can be nested within another loop. There is no real limit to the levels of nesting, other than in practicality of use. Similar to EMBEDDING and LEVELS. See also path.

NEST (Novell Embedded Systems Technology)
in NETWORK systems, a universal connectivity PROTOCOL for external DEVICES. NEST is used mainly in print and fax servers.

Net
short for the Internet.

netiquette
The informal rules of behavior that INTERNET users are encouraged to follow. Typical rules include: check with an FAQ list before asking a question, don't betray confidences, don't expect people to understand subtleties in EMAILS, stick to the subject you are writing about, don't use UPPERCASE in composing emails, etc, etc. There are several guides available online.

netizen
Literally "net citizen", someone who uses the Internet.

Netscape
A company founded in 1994 which produced software for the web, and the popular browser Navigator. It had an enormous impact on the market and came head on with Microsoft in the battle to dominate the browser market. Netscape also produces Communicator, a package or suite of programs that includes Navigator and additional items such as an HTML editor called Composer.

Netware

Netware
The Novell company's operating system for LOCAL AREA NETWORKS.

network
The interconnection of a number of terminals or computer systems by data communication lines. It may consist of two or more computers that can communicate between each other. Networks for PERSONAL COMPUTERS differ according to scope and size. LOCAL AREA NETWORKS (LANs) usually connect just a few computers (although it may be more than 50), perhaps in order that they can share the use of an expensive PERIPHERAL DEVICE. Large systems are called WIDE AREA NETWORKS and use telephone lines or similar media to link computers together. In general LANs cover distances of a few miles, and some of the largest versions are found in universities and large companies. Each user has a WORKSTATION capable of processing data, unlike the DUMB TERMINALS of a MULTIUSER system.

network administrator
The individual who is in charge of a LOCAL AREA NETWORK assisting users and ensuring the correct software is used.

network interface card
An adapter card that allows networking cable to be connected directly to the computer. MACINTOSH computers have a basic networking system built into the computer.

Network Neighborhood
A feature of Windows that appears as an icon and shows, when double-clicked, the extent of the network available

NIC

through the computer being used. It will show whatever computers, printers, etc. are linked to the network.

network operating system
The operating system that is used as a controller for all network components. The network operating system controls FILE SERVER software, the individual workstation software and the network hardware.

network server
see FILE SERVER; SERVER.

newbie
A first-time user of computers or of a particular ENVIRONMENT. The term is often used to describe newcomers to the INTERNET.

newsgroup
A group of Internet users who discuss a topic of mutual interest on an ongoing basis. Contributors to a newsgroup use a newsreader program to make a contribution (posting) to the newsgroup and read the contributions of others. Newsgroups can be moderated – they have an administrator who vets postings before they appear.

neXT
A computer workstation designed by Steve Jobs who was a founding member of APPLE COMPUTER. The computer uses the UNIX operating system with a GRAPHIC USER INTERFACE.

NIC
see NETWORK INTERFACE CARD.

nickel cadmium battery or NiCad battery

nickel cadmium battery or NiCad battery
A type of rechargeable battery used in NOTEBOOK and LAPTOP COMPUTERS.

nickel metal hydride battery
A rechargeable battery that is more powerful than the NICKEL CADMIUM BATTERY and so is more suitable for NOTEBOOK and LAPTOP COMPUTERS.

node
A connection point that joins two devices, such as the joining of a WORKSTATION to a NETWORK. The workstation is commonly referred to as a node of the network.

noise
Static that is caused by electrical interference and that can reduce the effectiveness of data communications. DIGITAL communication lines do not suffer interference in the way that ANALOG lines do.

non-impact printer
A PRINTER that produces text output on plain or special paper without contact between the printing mechanism and the paper. Typical examples are INKJET, bubblejet or LASER PRINTERS. Most are capable of high quality print.

Norton Utilities
A suite of UTILITY programs from Symantec Corporation, which include undelete options, performance testing programs, and so on.

NOT
see LOGICAL OPERATOR.

notebook computer
A small computer that is generally more compact than a LAPTOP. These are useful for mobile users but are not very satisfactory for sustained usage.

Novell
A corporation that specializes in software solutions for networks.

null modem cable
A cable used to connect two computers without using a MODEM. These cables are generally used to transfer files from a mobile computer, such as a notebook, to a desktop machine at an office to ensure that files are consistent between the computers.

num lock key
A keyboard key that when pressed fixes the keypad to NUMERIC FORMAT rather than the optional controls or characters.

numeric format
In a SPREADSHEET, the way a number can be displayed is controlled by use of the numeric format command. The number can be displayed in a variety of ways, including with no decimals; with two decimals; with currency prefix; as a date or time.

numeric keypad
A section of the keyboard that allows numbers to be entered in an easy format (*see* KEYPAD).

O

object
Any item that can be selected and manipulated; a self-contained module of DATA - the basis of OBJECT TECHNOLOGY; a block of data, text or graphics that was created by a separate APPLICATION.

In OBJECT-ORIENTED PROGRAMMING, an entity that consists of both data and the procedures to manipulate that data.

object code
A MACHINE LANGUAGE representation of programming SOURCE CODE, created by a COMPILER and then turned into executable code by a linker. *See also* OBJECT-ORIENTED PROGRAMMING.

object linking and embedding (OLE)
A set of STANDARDs designed to allow links to be created between documents and applications, thereby enabling information in one document to be automatically updated when the information in the other is changed.

object oriented font
see SCALABLE FONT.

object oriented graphics
The representation of a GRAPHICS image by a mathematical formula. In such a system, you can manipulate objects much more than with a BITMAP. Also, the higher the RESOLUTION of a monitor or printer, the sharper an object-oriented image will look, because the

image is *scalable*. This system is also know as VECTOR GRAPHICS. When FONTS are object-oriented, they are called OUTLINE FONTS, SCALABLE FONTS, or *vector fonts*. *See also* POSTSCRIPT; PCL; TRUETYPE.

object oriented programming system
A programming environment that consists of a range of objects that have their own programming code. The objects are incorporated into a program by combining them in the sequences required. A drawback with object oriented programming is that it operates slowly and uses a large amount of memory. It is, however, an easy way to be introduced to programming.

object technology
A form of SYSTEM design where systems are seen as chunks of DATA, known as objects, that consist of both data RECORDS and processing information, e.g. customer details plus all of the forms those details could be used for. A major aspect of object technology is the recycling of existing objects in new applications. The idea is that this is a more organic way of designing systems and one that makes it easier to upgrade and develop.

There has been a rapid growth in the development of this technology with the widespread availability of OBJECT-ORIENTED PROGRAMMING languages like JAVA and C++.

OCR
see OPTICAL CHARACTER RECOGNITION.

OEM (Original Equipment Manufacturer)
A business that makes a piece of hardware as opposed to the company that buys the hardware, reconfigures it,

off the shelf software

re-labels it and sells it to the end user. There may be only a few OEMs in the industry that make laser printer drivers but there may be many companies selling laser printers, many of which will have different features.

off the shelf software

A software application that is mass-marketed and serves a general purpose, rather than CUSTOM SOFTWARE, which is developed for a specific customer. (*See also* PACKAGED SOFTWARE.)

offline

equipment that is not under the direct control of the central processing unit. A printer may be in an offline state when it is switched on, but not capable of receiving data from the computer. This also applies to a mode of working with email and the Internet. While browsing the net, pages can be loaded and read later while offline. If you then want to follow a link not previously made, you will be prompted to reconnect. Files are stored in a temporary Internet files folder (if in Internet Explorer), which speeds up the process of revisiting a page.

offset

similar to GUTTER, it is the space added to a left margin to allow for the document binding.

OLE

see OBJECT LINKING AND EMBEDDING.

online

used when a computer is connected via a modem to an online service or Internet service provider. Using the computer in this way means the user is "online." Many computer software programs have online help. In place of bulky manuals, guidance and help can be sought through a help menu accessed by a button or command on the menu bar.

online community
see VIRTUAL COMMUNITY.

online help
A utility associated with a particular application that provides a help system for reference while the application is being operated.

online information service
A profit-making organization, such as AOL (America Online) or COMPUSERVE, that makes information available to its members or subscribers via telephone services. The online providers also provide CHAT FORUMS and libraries of information on a vast range of subjects.

online service (*see also* INTERNET SERVICE PROVIDER)
The term given to online services, such as technical support, chat rooms, games, and other facilities specific to the particular online service.

open
To access a file with its associated application in order to edit the file or print a hard copy of it.

open bus system
A design of the MOTHERBOARD where the expansion BUS has slots into which EXPANSION BOARDS can be fixed.

OpenGL (OPEN Graphics Language)

OpenGL (OPEN Graphics Language)
3-D graphics LANGUAGE that has become a standard for Windows, Macintosh and Unix computers. All high-end 3-D GRAPHICS ADAPTERS include OpenGL drivers.

operating environment
see ENVIRONMENT.

operating system
Every COMPUTER must have an operating system to be able to run other programs. Operating systems perform basic tasks, such as recognizing INPUT from the KEYBOARD, sending OUTPUT to the DISPLAY, keeping track of files and directories on the disk, and controlling PERIPHERAL devices. It makes sure that different programs running at the same time do not interfere with each other. The operating system is also responsible for security. Operating systems provide a PLATFORM, on top of which APPLICATIONS run. The applications have to be written for a particular operating system. For PCs, the most popular operating system is Windows, but others are available, such as Linux.

optical character recognition (OCR)
An information processing technology that can convert readable text into computer data. A SCANNER is used to import the image into the computer, and the OCR software converts the image into text. No single software package provides a foolproof conversion of text, but the more sophisticated ones have various means of highlighting queries and even recognizing certain unclear characters once the user has responded to the first case. It is a useful tool for inputting large amounts

orientation

of typewritten or already printed text for editing and changing.

optical disk

A type of disk that uses light to write data to the disk and read the data from the disk. It can hold large amounts of information but has slower access times than other SECONDARY STORAGE such as hard disks. CD ROMS use optical disk technology

optical fiber

A glass filament that is used to transmit data. Optical fibers can carry huge amounts of information over long distances and do not suffer from electrical interference, as do conventional copper wires.

optical mouse

An input device that is connected to a computer by light beams rather than wires. This allows the mouse more freedom on the user's desk.

option

A choice that the user faces when operating a computer. The simplest options appear in DIALOG BOXES where the choice of command is large but may be print, cancel, options or print preview.

OR

see FORMULA; LOGICAL OPERATOR.

orientation

Type can be laid down on a page in a vertical format (PORTRAIT ORIENTATION) or in a horizontal format

(LANDSCAPE ORIENTATION). Portrait orientation shows the page taller than it is wide and landscape orientation shows the page wider than it is tall.

OS/2

An operating system created by IBM, which brought a GRAPHICAL USER INTERFACE environment to the PERSONAL COMPUTER along with MULTITASKING and other advanced features.

outline font

Another way of describing a SCALABLE FONT. The CHARACTERS of the font are geometrically described by their outlines, which allows them to be extrapolated or interpolated, i.e. changed in size, by mathematical formula. Essentially, each character is a VECTOR GRAPHIC. *See also* POSTSCRIPT; TRUE TYPE.

outline utility

A UTILITY PROGRAM that is often incorporated in word processing programs and that allows the user to organize thoughts and concepts before creating a report.

output

most computer output comes in the form of printed reports, letters, etc, or information sent to a storage device. The most common output form, however, is the image on the screen. Output devices are peripherals that will accept information from the computer, such as a printer, external drive, floppy disk, CD or DVD.

output device

Any device that produces a usable form of output from

the computer. Printers produce a hard copy of files, documents, etc. A fax machine produces output to another fax machine. A screen (VDU) lets the user view output and a sound card allows the user to monitor sound output.

overtype mode
see INSERT MODE.

overwrite
To save a file on to a disk under a file name that already exists. The original file is deleted by being overwritten by the new version.

P

pack
To COMPRESS a file. It means saving files in a way that utilizes a minimum of disk space.

packaged software
Software that is mass-produced, marketed and sold. The software is the same for all users, unlike CUSTOM SOFTWARE, which is written specifically for a client. (*See also* OFF THE SHELF SOFTWARE).

packet
A block of DATA transmitted over a NETWORK in a *packet-switched system*.

packet switching
A technology used in networking in which a message is broken up into small segments or "packets" prior to transmission to addresses in a wide area network. Each segment contains the address of its destination and all the packets comprising a message do not necessarily have to travel along the same path, giving optimum use of available circuits in the network. The destination computer puts the component packets together to generate the message. Packet switching is suitable for data transmission but not for video; some public networks provide additional services, including email. *See also* circuit switching.

page
see WEB PAGE.

page break
A mark in a document that indicates the end of one page and the start of the next. A page break can be generated in a document by use of a menu or embedded command. The page break is extensively used in word processing or spreadsheet programs to provide the presentation required. *Soft page breaks* are placed automatically by a program, and as text is inserted, the page breaks move automatically. *Hard page breaks* are inserted into a document by the user and retain their position relative to the existing text.

page description language (PDL)
A high-level LANGUAGE for commanding a PRINTER to print text and GRAPHICS on a page. The two major examples are POSTSCRIPT and PCL. Both are object-oriented, meaning that they describe a page in terms of geometrical objects. *See also* VECTOR GRAPHICS.

page feed
see FEED.

page layout program
An application that allows the user to mix text and graphics in a document of virtually any page size and almost unlimited extent. Both text and graphics can be inserted from other software programs. DESKTOP PUBLISHING is made possible by page layout programs such as InDesign, PAGEMAKER and QUARK XPRESS.

page preview
A feature of many programs that shows the user the way a full page will appear in print. Page preview can show

PageMaker

exactly the format to be printed and will also allow checking of margins, headers and footers along with the placement of graphics.

PageMaker

A PAGE LAYOUT PROGRAM first published by Aldus. One of the pioneers of DESKTOP PUBLISHING, it is highly flexible and permits the incorporation of text and graphics into a document.

pages per minute (ppm)

A measurement of the number of pages that a printer can output per minute.

pagination

The process of dividing a document into pages and numbering the pages ready for printing.

paint program

A GRAPHICS application for creating images where the image is represented by a BITMAP (*bitmapped graphics*) and created by simulated painting on-screen, using the mouse or a GRAPHICS TABLET.

Unlike in a DRAW PROGRAM, a set of images created in one WINDOW in a paint program are not independent of each other. However, colors can be edited and various filters can apply a wide variety of special effects to areas of the images.

While draw programs allow for OBJECTS that can be manipulated independently, paint programs provide an electronic canvas to paint images onto. A commonly know example is Windows Paint. *See also* IMAGE EDITOR; RASTER.

palette
The menu of colors, brush styles or patterns that can be chosen to create an image in GRAPHICS programs.

pane
A term used for each section of a SPLIT SCREEN window. In SPREADSHEET programs a window can be split into four separate panes to make moving around it easier.

Pantone
A system that allocates numbers to a range of colors in order that the exact color match is made. The system is used by graphics studios and print shops to ensure that the color used in the printing is the color that the artist or designer requires.

paperless office
An office in which paper is no longer used or generated. Actually, the computer revolution has tended to produce more paper rather than less, but the era of the truly paperless office may be approaching.

parallel columns
A feature of word processing or page layout programs that sets two or more columns side by side.

parallel communication
see SERIAL COMMUNICATION.

parallel port
A port or slot on the back of a computer that is used to transmit high speed SYNCHRONOUS data streams. It is an

parallel printer

extension of a computer's internal DATA BUS and is used primarily for connection to printers.

parallel printer

A printer designed to be connected to a PARALLEL PORT. The printer cable connection should not be more than ten feet (three meters) long as the risk of interference increases with the length of the cable.

parallel processing

The use of two processors combined to undertake one task. The technique is used where there is a requirement for a massive number of calculations, such as in predicting the weather or high quality graphic processing. Parallel processing should be compared with MULTI-TASKING, which is the use of one processor to undertake two or more tasks simultaneously.

parameter

A step in any program sequence that will cause the program to take a specific course of action. It is a value that is added to a command to ensure the task is undertaken in the desired manner. For example, to format the disk in drive A one would type FORMAT A: and the A: is the parameter of the FORMAT command.

parent file

in a series of three BACKUPS of a file the parent file is the second oldest file. A conventional backup procedure is to keep three copies of important files. The first is the child, the next the parent and the oldest is the GRANDPARENT.

Pascal

parity bit
An extra BIT added to transmitted data that allows checking for communications errors. The parity bit is attached to each BYTE of data and indicates whether the sum of the bits is odd or even. When the receiving MODEM receives the data, a check is performed to ensure that the sum of the bits (odd or even) is the same as the parity bit. If not, an ERROR MESSAGE is reported.

park
To remove the READ/WRITE HEAD from a hard disk to an area of the disk that contains no data in order to protect files during transportation of the disk. If during transport the read/write head touches the surface of the disk there is the risk of data loss. The procedure to park the read/write heads can be achieved automatically or by using a *park utility* program each time the computer is to be moved.

partition
A section of a HARD DISK that is created for a particular purpose. A hard disk can be divided, or partitioned, into several parts. For example, one partition could hold the main OPERATING SYSTEM; a second could hold an alternative operating system such as UNIX. A third and fourth could contain data files relating to each operating system. The hard disk can also be partitioned for security purposes, with a PASSWORD required to access the different partitions.

Pascal
A HIGH-LEVEL COMPUTER PROGRAMMING LANGUAGE. It has waned in popularity with the advent of C. It was originally

passive matrix display

designed by Niklaus Wirth for the teaching of structured programming. It is used as a teaching language and in the development of applications. It is similar to BASIC in that the computer is told what to do by statements in the program. It is too slow for large-scale development, and commercial versions are changed sufficiently to make them individually isolated.

passive matrix display

A form of LCD screen display used for LAPTOP and NOTEBOOK COMPUTERS. A transistor is used to control an entire row or column of the display's electrodes. This type of display is cheap to produce and uses lower battery power than the more expensive but higher quality ACTIVE MATRIX DISPLAY, which uses a single transistor for each display electrode.

password

A key word that is selected by a user to protect files from unauthorized access.

password protection

A means of allowing files to be protected from unauthorized use. The password may be set up in such a way as to protect the file at different levels. For example, entry of the password could allow the user to read the file but not to edit it, or to have full access to edit and copy the file.

paste

A part of a "cut and paste" procedure in text editing by which a selection of text from a document is moved to or copied to a CLIPBOARD. Once the text is on the clipboard

pathname

it can be pasted or moved back to a selected area of the document.

patch

An addition to a computer software program that is released after the launch of the main product and which invariably serves to correct a fault (bug) or enhances the running of the program. Patches are common in gaming software to add new data to files.

path

A series of words and symbols that identifies the route to a FILE. In terms of file location, path is synonymous with *pathname*.

Every file has a NAME. Specifying this as the path, the OPERATING SYSTEM automatically looks for the file in the current WORKING DIRECTORY. However, if the file is in a different directory, you need to describe how to find it, by specifying the path that the system must follow.

Paths flow up or down the DIRECTORY STRUCTURE between the working directory and the ROOT DIRECTORY. They cannot flow sideways (i.e. laterally, within the same level). *See also* ABSOLUTE LINK; HYPERLINK; PATHNAME SEPARATOR; RELATIVE LINK; URL.

Path is also a DOS COMMAND, wherein you specify the directory location of EXECUTABLE FILES for specified operations.

Also, in general terms, the route between any two points in a system, whether referring to a line, a channel, a circuit or even data.

pathname

see PATH.

pathname separator

every OPERATING SYSTEM has its rules for specifying paths. In DOS, the ROOT DIRECTORY is identified by a BACKSLASH and each subdirectory is separated by an additional backslash. In MACINTOSH environments, directories are separated by a colon. In HTML, directories are separated by a forward slash, e.g. www.google.com/press/index.html. When ascending the DIRECTORY STRUCTURE, HTML uses "../" to signify a step up one level. *See* PATH; URL.

payment protocol

A PROTOCOL that governs online payments between a customer and a vendor. Security and reliability are the main aims. Currently, the *secure electronic payment protocol* and the SECURED ELECTRONIC TRANSACTION STANDARD are the main examples. *See also* DIGITAL MONEY.

PC (Personal Computer)

A MICROCOMPUTER that can be programmed to perform a variety of tasks for home and office. PCs can be equipped with all the necessary software and other devices to perform any task. They can be part of a large DATABASE or a small NETWORK. PCs are capable of performing computer-aided design tasks (*see* CAD) required by designers, architects engineers, etc, which formerly had to be performed on WORKSTATIONS and MINICOMPUTERS. The term PC is used to refer to IBM-compatible computers, i.e. those running DOS or WINDOWS operating systems as opposed to UNIX or MAC OS.

PC card

see PCMCIA.

PC DOS
The version of the disk operating system written by Microsoft Corporation that is packaged by IBM with their personal computers.

PCB (printed circuit board)
See CARD.

PCI (Peripheral Component Interconnect)
The most common INPUT/OUTPUT bus. The PCI BUS allows IRQs to be shared, which helps to solve the problem of limited IRQs and consequent CONFLICTs between PERIPHERALS. In a PCI machine, there cannot be insufficient IRQs, as all can be shared. This is the basis of PLUG AND PLAY.

PCL (Printer Control Language)
The PAGE DESCRIPTION LANGUAGE used in Hewlett Packard PRINTERS. It has become a STANDARD used by many manufacturers. Later levels support SCALABLE FONT technology.

PCMCIA (Personal Computer Memory Card International Association)
A group of manufacturers that has set a STANDARD for credit card-sized PERIPHERAL DEVICES such as memory cards, fax modems, sound cards, etc. The devices are designed primarily for NOTEBOOK COMPUTERS. The credit card-sized expansion cards originally referred to as PCMCIA cards are now more commonly referred to as PC cards.

PDA
see PERSONAL DIGITAL ASSISTANT.

PDF (Portable Document Format)

PDF (Portable Document Format)

document exchange FILE FORMAT developed by Adobe that can capture the formatting information of files from a variety of applications, which allows these documents to be displayed and printed on the recipient's monitor or printer, as per the original. To view a file in PDF format, you need the READER software, distributed for free by Adobe.

PDF files have *embedded fonts*, solving the problem of FONT INCOMPATIBILITY between computer systems. In addition, PDF files support POSTSCRIPT code. Consequently, PDF files are much used for sending material to commercial printers, as well as for publishing on the Web. *See* ADOBE ACROBAT; DOCUMENT EXCHANGE SOFTWARE; EMBEDDING; INTERNET PUBLISHING.

PDL

see PAGE DESCRIPTION LANGUAGE.

peer-to-peer

A network ENVIRONMENT where the computers in the NETWORK all act as SERVERS and share their files with each other. Peer-to-peer networks are commonly used in small organizations where a dedicated file server is not needed. In such cases, only specific folders are made sharable.

There are some services available on the Internet that allow users to access files on the computers of other remote users. This type of file sharing was how Napster worked. In essence, it is a global peer-to-peer network.

pen computer

A style of computer that can recognize handwriting as a

method of input. The computer has a touch-sensitive screen onto which the user writes with a pen-like device called a STYLUS. The computer interprets the writing and converts it to a digital form as if the input had been typed. Handwriting recognition software is constantly improving but still requires that the input writing is in the form of print rather than cursive writing.

Pentium
The name of a microprocessor chip from INTEL. The Pentium is a RISC that contains over three million transistors. It can operate at speeds of more than double that of its predecessor, the 486DX2 chip. (*See also* POWER PC.)

peripheral
A generic term for equipment that is connected to the computer. These are external (to the CENTRAL PROCESSING UNIT) and include such devices as external DISK DRIVES, PRINTERS, MODEMS, CD ROMS, SCANNERS and VDUS.

PERL (Practical Extraction and Report Language)
A PROGRAMMING LANGUAGE designed for processing text. Because of this, Perl has become one of the most popular languages for writing CGI scripts. It is an *interpretive language*, which makes it easy to build and test simple programs.

personal computer
see PC.

personal digital assistant (PDA)
A portable battery powered computer, slightly larger than

personal information manager

the palm of a hand, which is generally used for a small range of specific purposes such as note taking, address book, agenda calendar and to do lists.

Some PDAs have handwriting recognition systems, and most have the facility to use a fax, modem and PC card.

personal information manager
see PIM.

Phong shading
In computer GRAPHICS, a technique developed by Phong Bui-Tuong for computing a shaded surface. It is more realistic than GOURAUD SHADING, but is also more complex. It does not produce shadows or reflections. *See also* FLAT SHADING; RENDER.

PHP (PHP Hypertext Preprocessor)
A scripting LANGUAGE used to create DYNAMIC WEB PAGES. PHP code is embedded in HTML pages for server-side execution. It is commonly used to extract data from a database and present it on the web page.

physical drive
The hardware that is used as the storage device for a computer. A computer can have more than one physical drive. This can be compared with a logical drive, which could be a partition of a physical drive or a section of the RAM set aside to act as a storage area.

pica
A measure of FONT size equal to 12 POINTS (1/6 of an inch).

Ping

PICT (abbreviation for picture)
An object oriented graphics file format developed by Apple for the MacDraw program. The format uses separate GRAPHICS objects such as lines, rectangles, arcs and ovals, each of which can be independently moved or sized. A file saved in this format can be read by many programs.

pie graph
A form of graph used to present data in a visually attractive fashion. Pie charts are generally shaped like a circle and may have offset or exploded sections to highlight a particular figure.

PIF (Program Information File)
A file containing information about DOS applications that assists Microsoft WINDOWS in running the application. The file contains data such as the filename, how to display the file and the amount of memory to use. Windows can run a DOS application even if there is no PIF available.

PIM (Personal Information Manager)
SOFTWARE that organizes contact details, notes and diary information. It provides features such as automatic dialing, calendar, and scheduler. PIMs vary widely, but all provide methods for managing information easily.

pin feed
Similar to TRACTOR FEED.

Ping
A UTILITY that determines whether an IP ADDRESS is

piracy

accessible by sending a PACKET to the specified address and waiting for a reply. Ping is used to troubleshoot Internet connections.

piracy

The unauthorized copying of software, the rights of which belong to someone else. This is theft. (*See also* SOFTWARE PIRACY).

pitch

A measurement of the number of characters that a printer prints in a linear inch. Pica pitch uses 10 characters per inch while elite pitch uses 12 characters per inch.

pixel

A picture element that is the smallest dot that can be displayed on a screen. The pixels make up the picture to be displayed on screen.

plasma display

A type of display screen that uses charged gas particles to illuminates the screen.

platen

Part of the friction device that pulls paper through a printer. The platen also acts a solid surface from which the write head can impress the image onto the paper.

platform

Most often, a combination of the OPERATING SYSTEM and the HARDWARE, e.g. Windows and PC are seen as one platform (although this isn't really true). Also, very often used to differentiate MACINTOSH and PC systems. The term originally dealt with only hardware. The terms platform and ENVIRONMENT are synonymous.

platform independent
The description of a NETWORK that allows computers using different operating systems to be present.

plot
To create an image using lines rather than a series of dots.

plotter
A hardware device that creates drawings by moving a series of pens, usually of different colors, across a page. Plotters are commonly used in computer-aided design (*see* CAD) applications and other detailed graphic presentations.

Plug and Play
A technology that allows a PERIPHERAL DEVICE to be connected to a computer and then used without further setting of DIP SWITCHES. The computer will automatically create the necessary connections.

plug-in
A software MODULE that adds a feature or service to a larger APPLICATION. Usually, the plug-in refers to another major application. For example, ADOBE ACROBAT has a large number of plug-ins to other applications, such as Microsoft Word, that allows Acrobat operations to take place from within that application.

PNG

PNG
see PORTABLE NETWORK GRAPHICS.

point
The size of a FONT generated by a printer. There are 72 points in an inch. Normal fonts are printed at around 10 points. It also refers to the use of the mouse or other pointing device, such as a TRACKBALL, to position the CURSOR at a specific place on the screen. Additionally, it is to point to commands or data located in a separate record in a DATABASE MANAGEMENT PROGRAM.

point and click
A description of the process of using a device that POINTs, such as a MOUSE or TRACKBALL, to select a command. The user points to a menu command or file and clicks the mouse or trackball button once or twice and the command is selected or the file is opened.

pop-up menu
A menu of command options that appears on the screen when the user points and clicks a particular part of the screen or uses a second mouse button. (*See also* PULL DOWN MENU).

port
A plug or socket through which data may be passed into and out of a computer. Typically, each input and output device requires its own separate port. Most computers have a PARALLEL and a SERIAL PORT. The parallel port is a high-speed connection to printers while the serial port enables communication between the computer and serial printers, modems and other computers. In

addition to receiving and transmitting data, the serial port also guards against data loss.

portable computer
A computer that can be packed up and moved to a different location. (*See also* NOTEBOOK COMPUTER).

portable document format
see PDF.

portable network graphics (PNG)
BITMAP graphics file format that is expected to replace the GIF format. PNG provides advanced graphics features, such as 48-bit color, built-in color correction, tight compression and the ability to display and print at different resolutions. It has taken some time to get PNG off the ground.

portal
A general term for WEBSITES that provide a doorway to the Internet and to other services. Once, this was the province of the ISP home page, but now lots of organizations offer the same scale of services.

portrait orientation
A description of the normal way of printing a page of text. The page is longer than it is wide. (An A4 page is 297 x 210mm ($11^1/_2$ x $8^1/_4$ inches).

post
To add data to a record in a DATABASE MANAGEMENT PROGRAM or similar program, e.g. for keeping accounting records.

POST (Power On Self-Test)

POST (Power On Self-Test)
A test that a computer carries out on start-up to ensure that the main components are working correctly.

PostScript
An OBJECT-ORIENTED GRAPHICS language, wherein images, including fonts, are treated as collections of VECTOR GRAPHICS, rather than BITMAPS. PostScript FONTS are both OUTLINE FONTS and SCALABLE FONTS. With only one typeface definition, a PostScript printer can produce a multitude of fonts.

One advantage of vector graphics over bitmapped graphics is that the former is self-adjustable to the RESOLUTION of the OUTPUT DEVICE, whereas a bitmap has to be resampled in order to change its resolution. PostScript images are processed through a RASTER IMAGE PROCESSOR before being printed. Note that PostScript is a printing option. To save a file as PostScript, you have to PRINT TO FILE.

PostScript commands are LANGUAGE statements that are translated for (e.g.) the printer by an INTERPRETER in the printer. Every PostScript printer contains an interpreter. The language is known as a PAGE DESCRIPTION LANGUAGE. There are three basic versions of PostScript: Levels 1, 2 and 3.

ENCAPSULATED POSTSCRIPT handles graphic images in the PostScript format. *See also* ADOBE TYPE MANAGER; DRAW PROGRAM; SAMPLING.

power down
To turn off a computer. It is important to power down correctly, as most programs must be shut down in a proper sequence otherwise data may be lost or corrupted.

Power PC

A MICROPROCESSOR chip manufactured by Motorola and used by IBM and APPLE. It uses RISC technology and has the advantages of being relatively cheap to manufacture and consuming less power than other chips. (*See also* PENTIUM).

power supply

A device in a computer that converts the AC mains supply to DC current used by a computer. The power supply tends to be heavy and contributes greatly to the weight of a computer.

power up

To switch on a computer and load the OPERATING SYSTEM ready for use.

power user

A computer user who is able to use all the advanced features of a program or series of programs. A power user would be generally regarded as an expert.

ppm

see PAGES PER MINUTE.

precedence

The order in which arithmetic operations are performed. The order is important when creating formulae, e.g. in a computer program or spreadsheet. The rules of precedence are (1) exponential equations; (2) multiplication and division; (3) addition and subtraction. For example, the formula 6+5+9+8/4 does not give the average of the four numbers since the division is carried out before the additions. The result of the above is 22. In order to obtain the average of the four numbers, the formula must force the additions to be performed first. This is done with brackets as follows (6+5+9+8)/4, giving the correct average of 7.

Pretty Good Privacy (PGP)

A technique for encrypting messages and one of the most common ways to protect messages on the INTERNET, because it is effective, easy to use, and free. PGP is based on the PUBLIC KEY ENCRYPTION SYSTEM. To encrypt a message using PGP, you need the PGP encryption package, which is available for free from a number of sources.

PGP is such an effective tool that the US government actually brought a lawsuit against the DEVELOPER for making it available to "enemies" of the United States. The lawsuit was eventually dropped, but there are many restrictions in place regarding international use.

primary document

see CLIENT DOCUMENT.

primary storage

A computer's main RAM or ROM, unlike SECONDARY STORAGE such as hard disks, compact disks and optical disks.

print queue

A list of files to be printed that are temporarily held by a PRINT SPOOLER. The print spooler operating in the BACKGROUND sends each file in turn to the printer while the computer can operate normally in the FOREGROUND.

print spooler
A UTILITY PROGRAM that maintains a queue of files waiting to be printed. The print spooler sends a file to the printer whenever the printer is ready to receive another document.

print to file
An option in the print MENU that allows you to create a FILE that contains not only all the content of the original DOCUMENT, but also all the codes required to instruct a printer. The file can then be printed later, or elsewhere, without requiring the original APPLICATION. This is in fact the first thing a PRINT SPOOLER does, although the file is not saved. Note that the printer file (prn extension in Windows) is dependent on the DEVICE DRIVER, or LANGUAGE, used. See also EPS; POSTSCRIPT.

printed circuit board (PCB)
See CARD

printer
The device that produces hard copy. IMPACT PRINTERS, which operate by striking an ink ribbon onto paper to produce an image have been overtaken by NON-IMPACT PRINTERS, which make no contact with the paper.

printer control language
see PCL.

printer font
A FONT that a printer keeps in memory and uses to produce output on a page. The printer fonts sometimes differ from the display fonts used on screen, but with

printer port

TRUE-TYPE and POSTSCRIPT, the display fonts are the same as the printer fonts.

printer port
A port or slot on the computer to which a printer is connected. The port may be a SERIAL or a PARALLEL PORT.

private key
The private part of a two-part, PUBLIC KEY ENCRYPTION SYSTEM. The private key is always kept secret.

private network
A NETWORK that is only available to specified users, usually employees or members of an organization. It is often, but does not have to be, connected to the INTERNET, and can be restricted to one geographical site, or not. It may also allow REMOTE ACCESS. A private network based upon a WEB SERVER is known as an INTRANET. *See also* SERVER; FIREWALL; LAN; WAN.

procedure
see ROUTINE.

process colors
The four colors used in process printing – cyan (blue), magenta (red), yellow and black. In reproducing an image in print, any color can be recreated by a particular combination of these process colors. Each color is printed separately via a COLOR SEPARATION onto the same place on a piece of paper, the amount of ink printed determined by the SCREEN and the RESOLUTION. *See also* CMYK; COLOR REPRODUCTION; DITHERING.

processing
The normal operation of the computer acting upon the input data according to the instructions of the program in use.

processor
A device in computing that can perform arithmetical and logical operations.

program
A set of instructions arranged for directing a digital computer to perform a desired operation or operations. Programmers use a variety of HIGH-LEVEL PROGRAMMING LANGUAGES such as BASIC, C and FORTRAN to create programs (*see* PROGRAM LANGUAGE). At some stage the program is converted to MACHINE LANGUAGE so that the computer can carry out the instructions.

programmable
something is programmable if it is capable of receiving instructions to perform a specific task. A computer is programmable since you can instruct, or program it, to perform a variety of tasks.

programmer
someone who designs and writes the CODE of a PROGRAM. There are SYSTEM programmers and APPLICATION programmers. *See also* DEVELOPER; SOFTWARE ENGINEER.

programming
The procedure involved in writing instructions that the computer will follow to perform a specific task. Programming is part art and part science. The process can be summarized as follows:

programming language

1. decide on the purpose of the application.
2. collect and write down all the important factors and variables, using flow charts to depict the decision processes.
3. translate the ideas into a programming language.
4. compile the program to convert it into machine language that is understood by the computer.
5. test and eliminate errors from the program.
6. over a period of time make adjustments to enhance the program.

programming language

A language that is used by computer programmers to write computer routines, e.g. COBOL, BASIC, FORTRAN, PASCAL, C, Visual Basic. The HIGH-LEVEL PROGRAMMING LANGUAGES, such as BASIC, C, Pascal, are so called because the programmer can use words and arrangements of words that resemble human language, and this leaves the programmer free to concentrate on the program without having to think of how the computer will actually carry out the instructions. The language's COMPILER or INTERPRETER then turns the programmer's instructions into MACHINE LANGUAGE that the computer can follow.

prompt

A symbol or message that informs the user that the computer is ready to accept data or input of some form. A prompt could be "Are you sure you want to quit the program?" Yes or No. A more common prompt in DOS is C:>, which tells you that the computer is waiting for input.

proportional sizing
The process by which the user changes the size of a GRAPHICS object without altering the relative dimensions of the image.

proportional spacing
A font in which each letter takes up space relative to the size of that letter. For example, the letter m takes up more space than the letter i. This compares with a MONOSPACE font, which allocates the same space to each letter.

proprietary
A term for technology that is developed and owned by a person or company who restricts the use of the technology. If anyone wants to use that technology a fee or license has to be negotiated.

protocol
The conventions or rules that govern how and when messages are exchanged in a communications network or between two or more devices. There are many different protocols, but communicating devices must use the same protocols in order to exchange data.

proxy server
A SERVER that helps to implement a FIREWALL in a NETWORK. The proxy server acts as a secure FRONT END to a vulnerable server. If a CRACKER wanted to infiltrate the network, they would have to deal with the proxy server first. Note that the proxy server could also simply act as a means of rapidly delivering WEB PAGES to an external ADDRESS.

public domain software

public domain software
A computer program that is distributed free to users.

public key
The publicly-known half of a two-part, PUBLIC KEY ENCRYPTION SYSTEM. The private part is known only to the owner.

public key encryption system
A cryptographic system that uses two keys – a PUBLIC KEY, and a PRIVATE KEY known only to the message recipient. The former can be made available to parties other than the sender or receiver. The public key is used to encrypt a message; the private key to decrypt it. The advantage of this form of transmission is that there is no need to use secure transmission. The disadvantage is that it is much slower then, for instance, SYMMETRIC KEY ENCRYPTION. Communication over the Internet tends to be two-way , so, in practice, two sets of public and private keys are usually employed by the sender and recipient of messages. Public key encryption is used for short messages or for transmitting the secret keys used in symmetric key encryption. The SECURE SOCKETS LAYER uses public key encryption to send the keys for the symmetric key encryption used for sending secure data. *See also* ENCRYPTION; DECRYPTION; DIGITAL CERTIFICATE.

pull-down menu
A selection of sub-options related to a command name on the main menu bar. For example, a style command on the main menu bar could have the sub-options of bold, italic, underline, double underline, superscript, subscript, text color.

Q

Quark XPress
A PAGE LAYOUT PROGRAM, published by Quark Inc, used as a standard by most newspaper publishers, and main rival to PAGEMAKER.

query
in a DATABASE MANAGEMENT PROGRAM, a query is when the user asks the program to find a particular reference or type of data that is in the records of the database.

queue
when two or more files are waiting for an action to take place. For example, in a LOCAL AREA NETWORK several users may send files to the printer for output. Each print job is added to a queue and is processed in turn.

quit
To exit from a program. It is important to quit from a program in a proper fashion, i.e. through the correct menu command, as failure to do this could result in loss of data or program preferences.

QWERTY
The standard typewriter/computer keyboard, denoted by the letters on the top line of characters. It was originally developed to slow down typists to stop the manual typewriters jamming the keys. There are now other alternatives to QWERTY keyboards that enable faster use and easier learning. One such system is the DVORAK KEYBOARD, which places the most frequently used letters together.

R

RAD

see RAPID APPLICATION DEVELOPMENT.

radio button

A round button that allows the user to choose one of a range of OPTIONS in a DIALOG BOX. Option buttons differ from CHECK BOXES in that several options can be checked in check boxes but only one radio button option can be chosen.

RAID (Redundant Array of Independent/ Inexpensive Disks)

A category of DISK DRIVES that employ two or more drives in combination. RAID drives are often used on SERVERS.

RAM (Random Access Memory) or main memory or internal memory

The memory that can be, and is, altered in normal computer operations. The RAM stores program instructions and data to make them available to the CENTRAL PROCESSING UNIT (CPU), and the CPU can write and read data. Application programs use a part of the RAM as a temporary place of storage, allowing modification of the file in use until it is ready for storage permanently on disk. Any work in the RAM that has not been saved will be lost if the power fails.

RAM cache

A part of the RAM that is set aside to store data and programs in order that the computer can operate more speedily. The computer processor can transfer data and program code to and from the RAM cache many times faster than it can transfer data and program code to and from a hard disk. If the CENTRAL PROCESSING UNIT had to wait on the hard disk to complete an operation there would be no point in having faster processors.

RAM disk

An area of RAM set aside by a UTILITY PROGRAM that is formatted to act like a disk drive. The RAM disk is volatile, and the contents will be lost when the computer is shut down. There is a significant advantage in speed to be gained from using a RAM disk, but it is important to ensure that data is stored onto a floppy or hard disk on a regular basis to avoid the risk of data loss.

random access

The retrieval of information randomly from any part of the computer memory or from magnetic media, which means that the computer can reach the information straight away without having to go through a series of locations to reach the desired point.

random access memory

see RAM.

range

A CELL or a group of contiguous cells in a SPREADSHEET program. A range of cells could include a ROW, part of a row, a COLUMN, a part of a column or a group of cells spanning several rows and columns. Ranges are usually given names that relate to the information contained in the range. For example, the range D5.. D9 might contain sales for a division of a business and could be given the name "salesdiv1". Any future reference in a formula to the range D5.. D9 could use "salesdiv1", e.g. Sum(salesdivl).

rapid application development (RAD)

A system that allows DEVELOPERS to build APPLICATIONS quickly, using special TOOLs to build USER INTERFACEs that would normally take a large effort. RAD employs a variety of design and development tools, including VISUAL PROGRAMMING and GUI builders, that get prototypes up and running quickly. Two of the most popular RAD systems for Windows are Visual Basic and Delphi.
Also, a project method where working parts of the project are delivered and implemented every few months, rather than waiting until the entire project is finished. This avoids premature obsolescence, but threatens the creation of a never-ending project. *See also* PROGRAMMING; RAPID PROTOTYPING.

rapid prototyping

Taking a computer-designed 3-D model and turning it into a physical object, via a prototyping machine, such as a laser etcher. There are machines that can build prototypes from various materials, such as paper and liquid polymer. *See also* CAD/CAM, RAD.

raster

A form of computer-graphic presentation in which the image is composed of a matrix of dots or pixels. Otherwise known as bitmaps, or bitmapped images, there are several file formats that use raster graphics, including TIF, BMP, PCX. The same technology is used in computer monitors and television sets.

raster display
The type of display found in TV sets. An electron beam scans the screen many times a second, moving in a zigzag pattern down the screen. Each horizontal line is made up of dots that are lit up individually to create a pattern

raster image processor
see RIP.

ray tracing
In computer GRAPHICS, a rendering technique for simulating light reflections, refractions and shadows in an image. Ray tracing works by simulating the path of a ray of light as it is absorbed or reflected by the various objects in the image. Ray tracing requires a lot of processing power, and is supported only by advanced graphics APPLICATIONS. *See also* RENDER; TEXTURE MAPPING.

RDRAM (Rambus DRAM)
An extremely fast dynamic RAM chip technology. Concurrent RDRAMs have been used in video games, while Direct RDRAMs are used in computers.

read
To retrieve information stored on magnetic media and transfer it to the memory of the computer.

read only attribute
information stored in a file's directory that tells the computer whether or not the file can be modified or deleted. If the file is read only, it cannot be changed in any way.

read only memory

read only memory
see ROM.

read.me file
A text file that is often included with program disks and contains up-to-date information about the program, provides updates to the program's instruction manual or gives technical hints or tips about the operation of the program.

read/write
Capable of being read and of being written to. Generally, it refers to MEMORY storage and types of DISK and disk drive, e.g. CD-R.

read/write head
The electromechanical means whereby information stored on magnetic media can be retrieved and transferred to the memory of the computer.

read/write head alignment
A DISK DRIVE must be correctly set up otherwise it may not be able to read a disk correctly. Incorrect alignment may be caused by jolting the computer during transport.

reader
A DEVICE that captures DATA and inputs it to the computer, e.g. an OPTICAL CHARACTER RECOGNITION reader, a magnetic card reader or a BARCODE reader.

Also, a PROGRAM that *reads* specific sorts of data, particularly in DOCUMENT EXCHANGE SOFTWARE. *See also* Adobe ACROBAT; FILE VIEWER.

recalculation order

real time
The near-instantaneous processing of data and feedback so that the user can respond immediately to the computer program. Programs that use real time processing include flight simulator games, online chat forums and point-of-sale recording.

real-time clock
An electronic circuit that maintains the time of day. It is usually self-adjusting for daylight saving, etc.

reboot
To restart the computer without turning off the power. The computer's primary RAM memory is initialized and the operating system is reloaded.
See also BOOT.

recalculation method
The selected method chosen to recalculate a SPREADSHEET after the values in a CELL or number of cells have been changed. The spreadsheet can be automatically recalculated or it can be manually recalculated when the user commands.

recalculation order
The sequence that a SPREADSHEET program uses to calculate a spreadsheet. When spreadsheets first appeared, the method of recalculation was restricted to COLUMN-wise or ROW-wise, i.e. the calculation proceeded down one column before moving to the next column. This produced some errors if the spreadsheet logic was not well thought out. More recent spreadsheets use a natural recalculation method that scans the sheet to find

record

the logical recalculation order and calculates a CELL only once all dependent cells have been calculated.

record

To store data on a disk. Also, all the information related to a topic in a database of information. For example, in a database of customers of a business a record will contain all the relevant information about one customer

recover

To restore lost or damaged files. The files can be recovered by restoring from a BACKUP copy or undulating the file. The backup may not have the most recent changes recorded, and so the full, up-to-date information may not be recovered. The undelete method depends on the information on the disk not having been overwritten. UTILITY PROGRAMS that undelete files are commercially available.

redlining

The process of marking changes or additions to the text of a document when comparing different versions. The circuitry and devices that are capable of storing data as well as programs. Memory must be installed in all modern computer systems. It is the computer's primary storage area, e.g. RAM (random access memory) as distinguished from the secondary storage of disks. Typical memory devices are SIMMs, Single In-line Memory Modules, which are plugged into the motherboard of the computer.

reformat

To repeat a FORMATTING operation on a disk or to proceed

relational operator

with a formatting operation on a disk that has already been formatted. In word processing, page layout or spreadsheet program, to reformat means to change the arrangement or style of the text.

refresh
To update the image on the computer screen. The screen is being constantly updated by an electron gun firing electrons at the phosphorous screen. When the computer processor sends a change to the video output it must be reflected on the screen. Each time the screen is refreshed it will reflect the changes.

refresh rate
The speed at which the monitor updates its display.

registry
DATABASE used by the Windows OPERATING SYSTEM to store configuration information. Most Windows applications write data to the Registry. You can edit the registry directly.

relational database
A type of DATABASE MANAGEMENT PROGRAM in which data is stored in two-dimensional tables that are indexed for cross-reference. Reports can be created using data from two files that are related in a particular way.

relational operator
A sign that is used to specify the relationship between values. Relational operators are used in queries on databases. For example, to obtain a report on transactions between two dates an expression such as:

relative cell reference

=>"1/12/95" & =<"31/12/95"

will extract a list of transactions from December 1 through 31, 2001. Other relational operators are:

- =   equal to
- <   less than
- >   greater than
- <=   less than or equal to
- >=   greater than or equal to
- <>   not equal to

relative cell reference

A reference to a CELL in a SPREADSHEET that refers to its position with regard to another cell rather than an absolute reference.

relative link

A HYPERLINK that references a PATH to a TARGET file, where the current WORKING DIRECTORY is the implied ROOT DIRECTORY and the file is referenced with respect to the folder which contains it. Moving (i.e. cutting or copying) the directory (along with all subdirectories) will not change the path.

release number

The decimal number that is used to identify an improvement in a version of a software program.

remote access

logging onto a NETWORK from a distant location, using a COMPUTER, a MODEM or BROWSER, and some remote access software to connect to the network. The only difference between a remote HOST and a network TERMINAL is slower data transfer speed. *See also* DIAL-UP NETWORKING.

removable storage
Any SECONDARY STORAGE system where the storage medium can be extracted and taken away from the computer. Magnetic tapes, floppy disks and disk cartridges are examples of removable storage.

rename
To change the name of a file, directory or disk.

render
To convert a FILE (or any DATA) to the FORMAT required for DISPLAY or print; to make visible the finished result; to produce.

In art, a rendering is an artist's representation of an object or view.

In computer GRAPHICS, the process of adding realism to an image by adding certain qualities, such as shadows. One technique is RAY TRACING; another type is SCANLINE RENDERING. There is also basic lighting, such as GOURAUD SHADING, as well as more sophisticated effects, including the application of textures to surfaces. *See* RAPID PROTOTYPING; TEXTURE MAPPING.

repaginate
documents are divided into pages for reporting purposes and when text is added to a page the division between the pages is changed. For the user to see where PAGE BREAKS occur, the document must be repaginated. Some programs repaginate the document automatically.

repeat rate
The rate at which a character will be typed on the screen when a particular key is kept depressed.

report

report
A presentation of information in print. The report will be complete with page numbers, footers and headers. It will be formatted in such a way as to make it attractive and easy to read.

reset button
A button on a computer (often on the front panel) that allows the user to perform a WARM BOOT or restart of the computer. It does not switch the computer off. (*See also* BOOTSTRAPPING.)

resolution
A measurement of the sharpness of an image generated by a printer or VDU. Printer resolution is measured in DOTS PER INCH. The more dots per inch, the greater the sharpness of the image on the paper. VDU resolution is measured in the number of PIXELs and their size. The smaller the pixel and the more there are on screen, the greater the resolution of the image. (*See also* DESKTOP PUBLISHING, DOT PITCH, HIGH RESOLUTION, LOW RESOLUTION).

resources
describes the available processing power of the COMPUTER at any given time, when all current operations have been taken into account.

restore
To recreate the conditions or state of a disk, file or program before an error or event occurred to destroy or corrupt the data. Restoration would normally involve use of a BACKUP file made previously.

retrieve
To obtain data previously stored on file in order that work can be done on the data.

return
A COMMAND KEY on the keyboard that is used to initiate a chosen command.

reverse video
A state in monochrome monitors in which instead of black text on a white background displays white text on a black background.

RGB (Red, Green, Blue)
video display devices use a color model called RGB, in which all colors can be represented by a mixture of the three *additive primary colors*. In order to do this, in the case of a CRT display, three electron guns inside the VDU represent each primary and their beams converge on each PIXEL to produce a color combination.

It is necessary to compare RGB and CMYK colors and convert one to the other so that what gets printed looks the same as what appears on the MONITOR. This is known as *color matching*. See also COLOR REPRODUCTION.

rich text format
A STANDARD relating to the creation of a TEXT FILE in a way that the FORMATTING details are available to other programs. Use of the standard allows files to be transported between applications, possibly by telephonic communication, without loss of the format of the text.

right click

right click
In WINDOWS, the right-hand MOUSE button enables you to quickly accomplish common tasks. If you click an item by using the right button, a MENU is displayed containing commands specific to the item. You can still use the left-hand button and menus to complete these same tasks.

It is possible to get the MACINTOSH to do something similar by pressing "control" as you click the mouse.

right justification
The alignment of text in a word processing document along the right margin of the document.

ring back systems
A security system for communications over telephone lines. When the system answers a call from a remote computer system, it confirms the identity of the remote computer and returns the call using a pre-stored telephone number. Unauthorized access to the main computer is therefore restricted and only authorized users can communicate in this way.

RIP (Raster Image Processor)
software and/or hardware that turns VECTOR GRAPHICS into a BITMAP, allowing it to be printed. This is most common with POSTSCRIPT, where the RIP has to translate the whole of a document. Printers generally are supplied as PostScript compliant, or not. Increasingly, software RIPs are being adopted – they are more flexible, and they are quicker. *See also* ADOBE TYPE MANAGER.

RISC (Reduced Instruction Set Chip)
A chip that has a limited number of instructions that

the processor can execute, thus increasing the speed of the PROCESSOR. The processor is designed to emphasize the most common instructions and to allow these instructions to work as fast as possible.

robot

An electromechanical device that may perform programmed tasks. Robots are commonly used in automated factories to perform repetitive functions. The first industrial robots were developed in the early 1960s, although they consisted of little more than an automated hand.

ROM (Read Only Memory)

The part of a computer's internal memory that can be read but not altered. It contains the essential programs (system programs) that neither the computer nor the user can alter or erase. The instructions that enable the computer to start up come from the ROM, although the tendency now is to put more of the operating system on ROM chips, rather than putting it on disk.

root

Another name for a SOURCE. The top level of a HIERARCHY.

root directory

in a HIERARCHICAL FILE SYSTEM, the top directory LEVEL. When the computer is *booted*, the root directory is the WORKING DIRECTORY. Access to subdirectories requires the naming of a PATH. *See also* ABSOLUTE LINK.

router

A DEVICE that forwards DATA packets along networks from

routine

one NETWORK to another. A router is connected to at least two networks, commonly two LANs, or WANs, or a LAN and its ISP network. Routers are located at GATEWAYS, the places where two or more networks connect. These devices are becoming more common in the home, where it is desired to share a BROADBAND Internet connection between several computers.

routine

A set of instructions that allow a task to be performed by a PROGRAM. Programs consist of modules, each of which contains one or more routines. The term is synonymous with PROCEDURE and FUNCTION. SUBROUTINE is, as it implies, a nested routine. *See* LOGIC PATH; NEST; PROGRAMMING

row

In a SPREADSHEET program a row is a horizontal block of CELLS that extends from the left to the right of the spreadsheet. The row is usually identified by an alphanumeric character.

RTF

see RICH TEXT FORMAT.

ruler

In a word processing environment, a bar at the top of the page to assist the user in setting margins and tab stops.

run

To initiate or execute a program. The computer reads the code from the disk and stores all or part of the code in the RAM. The computer can then perform tasks.

runtime
occurring during the actual execution of a program.

runtime version
A special version of an INTERPRETER that allows one application only to be run. For example, a program may have been written in PASCAL and will require a Pascal interpreter. However, the user may not have a Pascal interpreter in his or her computer system. The solution is that the program has its own limited or special interpreter that will work only with that program.

S

S/MIME (Secure Multimedia Internet Mail Extensions)
A STANDARD for secure email that uses a DIGITAL CERTIFICATE and hence requires some form of CERTIFICATE AUTHORITY to make it work. It works well with PRETTY GOOD PRIVACY. *See also* MIME; ATTACHMENT.

sampling
Digitizing ANALOG information; the creation of a DIGITAL image from an analog image.

Also, a technique used to capture analog events, wherein "samples" of the event are recorded regularly. If the *sampling rate* is fast enough, the human eye cannot see the gaps between the samples. This is how video and movies work.

It is possible to change the fundamentals of a digital "recording" in a limited way. With a BITMAP, for instance, one can decrease the RESOLUTION or size of the image, or both. Increasing the size will degrade the image resolution. Increasing the resolution can only be done by decreasing the physical size of the image in PIXELS. This process is called *resampling*.

sans serif
A plain type style or FONT, such as Helvetica, that has no detail at the end of the main character stroke.
This is sans serif text
This is serif text

save

To transfer the contents of a computer's RAM to a less volatile memory such as a HARD DISK or FLOPPY DISK. It is recommended that work is saved at regular intervals otherwise there is the risk of losing work if the RAM memory is deleted. This can happen if there is a power supply failure or a system CRASH.

scalable font

A FONT created in an OBJECT-ORIENTED GRAPHICS language. The printed BITMAPS are generated from a set of mathematical representations of the typeface, so the font can be created in any required size. An added advantage in that the greater the resolution of a printer or monitor, the better a scalable font will look. Scalable fonts are also called *object-oriented fonts* or *vector fonts*. The two major scalable font formats are POSTSCRIPT and TRUETYPE.

scalable vector graphics (SVG)

A VECTOR GRAPHICS file format that displays images in XML pages. In contrast to bitmapped JPEG and GIF images on the web, SVG images are scalable and adjust in size and RESOLUTION according to the open WINDOW. SVG files are smaller in size than GIF and JPEG files, support complex animation and, importantly, allow font EMBEDDING in web pages.

Developed by W3C, SVG is also available for use by mobile phones and other handheld devices in the form of SVGB (= Basic) and SVGT (= Tiny). *See also* GRAPHICS FILES; WEB DESIGN.

scaling

in presentation graphs, the *y*-axis can be scaled to

scanline rendering

produce a GRAPH that displays the data in a more visually pleasing form or in a way that emphasizes the results being depicted on the graph.

scanline rendering

A 3-D computer GRAPHICS rendering method that works on a point-by-point basis. A point on a line is calculated, followed by successive points on the line. When the line is finished, rendering proceeds to the next line. Scanline rendering is used by most modern graphics CARDS.

See also *RENDER*.

scanned image

Any image that has been DIGITIZED by a SCANNER and converted to a BITMAP.

scanner

A piece of hardware that copies an image or page into a computer by creating a DIGITAL image. A scanner works by bouncing a beam of light off the paper and recording the reflected light as a series of dots similar to the original image. If the dots are created as a variation of 16 gray values, the scanner is using a tagged image file format (*see* TIFF), otherwise a dithered image is created (*see* DITHERING). This is a simulation of a HALFTONE image, which is created by varying the size of, and the space between, the dots to create the image. Digital halftones become distorted when they are sized. Scanners are available in three basic types: a drum scanner, a FLATBED SCANNER or a HAND-HELD SCANNER. *See also* COLOR SEPARATION.

schema

The definition of the structure and content of a DATABASE.

The definition of the content of an XML document. The schema is embedded in the document. *See also* XSD; DOCUMENT TYPE DEFINITION.

scrapbook
A UTILITY PROGRAM that can be used to retain frequently used images, pictures, or text.

screen
Another name for the VDU, DISPLAY or MONITOR.

It is also, in the reproduction of images for print, a VIRTUAL or physical mesh through which the image is captured. As a result, the image is transformed from CONTINUOUS TONE into HALFTONE, where it is made up of dots, the density of which corresponds to the density of the image area. The fineness of the screen is most often expressed in DOTS PER INCH – the higher the dpi, the higher the RESOLUTION of the image. Screens also have a mesh angle – in four-color work, the differing angle of the screen for each color results in a "color rose" being printed for each dot position, thus creating a rendition of the color original. In computing parlance, this process is known as DITHERING. *See also* COLOR REPRODUCTION; COLOR SEPARATION; CMYK; CAPTURE; CONTINUOUS TONE; RGB.

screen capture
To take a "snapshot" of the screen at a particular moment. The snapshot can then be used to explain an entry in a technical manual or dictionary of terms.

screen dump
A printed output of a snapshot of the screen.

screen font

screen font
A FONT that is used by a program to display text. ADOBE TYPE MANAGER and TRUETYPE fonts produce screen fonts that are SCALABLE and produce exactly the same design in printed output.

screen saver
A UTILITY PROGRAM that is designed to prolong the life of a screen by switching off the image after a period of non-use.

script
A list of instructions that automatically perform a task within an application program. The script is a program within a program but can easily be written by automatically recording a series of keystrokes. For example, a user manually enters the commands, telephone numbers and passwords to allow entry to an online information service. Once the user is logged on, the keystrokes to retrieve certain information are recorded. The final sequence to log off is also recorded. The next time that the information is to be retrieved from the online service the script can be selected to control the process automatically.

scroll
To move the ACTIVE WINDOW over a document so that a different part of the document is visible in the window. Scrolling can be vertical or horizontal. In a word processing document scrolling vertically allows sight of the various pages in the document. Horizontal scrolling allows sight of a horizontally oriented spreadsheet.

SCSI (Small Computer System Interface)
An INTERFACE connection that allows high speed transfer

of information between a computer and one or more peripherals such as hard disks, scanners, or printers. The devices can be connected in a chain so that one SCSI port can support several devices at a time, although data can only be transferred from one device at a time.

SDRAM (Synchronous DRAM)
A *dynamic RAM* memory chip, based on standard dynamic RAM chips, but having features that make them considerably faster.

SDSL (Symmetric Digital Subscriber Line)
A technology that allows more DATA to be sent over existing copper telephone lines, SDSL supports data rates up to 3 Mbps. SDSL cannot operate simultaneously with voice connections over the same wires. A special MODEM is required. SDSL is symmetric because it supports the same data rates for upstream and downstream traffic.

See also ADSL.

search engine
A fundamental facility or tool that is used to look for and retrieve information on the web. Search engines use a program to look around the web and bring back information pertaining to the topic requested. The program used, often called a spider program, follows links on pages and the search engines store data derived from the HTML header text and meta tags. A specific search then looks through all the derived data to present its results. Some of the better known search engines are: AltaVista, Lycos, Yahoo, and Google.

second generation

second generation
The era in computing technology that is represented by use of transistors rather than vacuum tubes in computing devices. This generation was evident in the early 1960s and was superseded by the THIRD GENERATION, when INTEGRATED CIRCUITS replaced the transistor.

secondary storage or auxiliary storage
A form of permanent storage of data on disk drives. The drives can be HARD DISKS, magnetic tapes, FLOPPY DISKS, CD ROMs or OPTICAL DISKS. The main feature of secondary storage is that it is not deleted when the computer's power is turned off.

sector
A storage area on a disk. When a disk is formatted it is organized into TRACKS and sectors. A sector is a pie-shaped division of the magnetic surface on the disk that separates information into individual sections or zones. Data can be stored in these sectors and read by the disk drive. A unit of storage of one or more sectors is called a cluster.

secure HTTP
An extension to the HTTP PROTOCOL to support secure DATA transmission over the Internet. It is not currently supported by all browsers and servers - SSL is much more popular. The two protocols, however, have very different designs - whereas SSL is designed to establish a secure connection between two computers, S-HTTP is designed to secure the individual messages.

secure server
A WEB SERVER that supports any of the major security

security

protocols that protect the DATA against being violated. This means that data from your BROWSER is encrypted before being uploaded to the WEBSITE, making it difficult for a third party to decipher.

The term also refers to a web server that is protected against attack from the INTERNET in the form of a VIRUS, or hackers and crackers. *See also* ANTI-VIRUS PROGRAM; FIREWALL; CRACK; HACKER; SERVER.

secure site
See SECURE SERVER.

secure sockets layer
See SSL.

secure URL
A UNIFORM RESOURCE LOCATOR associated with SSL, identifying a SECURE SITE or PAGE.

Secured Electronic Transaction Standard
Applied to DIGITAL CERTIFICATES, which provide authentication for credit card purchases over the Internet, this PAYMENT PROTOCOL was developed by several major credit card companies, including Visa and MasterCard. *See also* DIGITAL MONEY.

security
The method of protecting files or programs so that unauthorized people cannot copy, access, or damage them. There are several methods of securing files, including the use of a PASSWORD, physically locking the computer, the use of data ENCRYPTION, or by downloading files to removable disks for safe storage.

seek

seek

To locate a file on a disk. A FILE ALLOCATION TABLE indicates the part of the disk on which the file or program is stored. The READ/WRITE HEADS are directed to the correct location, and the information is read to the processor. The time that it takes for the read/write heads to reach the correct sector is called the *seek time*.

select

To chose a portion of a document or database in which to perform a particular task or to review the selected records.

serial communication

A method of transferring data over a single wire, one BIT at a time. Data can be transferred over a relatively long distance using serial communications compared with parallel communication, which is restricted to a distance of around ten feet (three meters) because of the problems of interference.

serial mouse

An input pointing device that is connected to a serial port on the computer as opposed to the bus mouse, which is connected to the main processor board.

serial port

A PORT on the back of a computer that is set up to allow SERIAL COMMUNICATIONS between the computer and another device.

serial printer

A printer that connects to a serial port of the computer. The serial printer is slower than a parallel printer but can be

set up

sited at the other end of the office whereas the parallel printer must be within about ten feet (three meters) of the computer.

serif
The detailed strokes at the end of the main strokes of a character. Times is a FONT with serifs. (*See also* SANS SERIF.)

server
A computer used in a local area network that is the main source of programs or shared data. The server also controls the use of peripherals such as printers or modems by creating queues of requests that are answered in a sequential order. In Internet terminology, a server is any computer that can make access online to an external source, making services available to a network. *See also* CHAT SERVER; WEB SERVER.

service provider
A company that provides a connection to the INTERNET in return for a monthly subscription and a charge per hour of use. The service provider may facilitate a simple connection or may make available added services such as news and sports services, online shopping, etc. *See also* IAP; ISP.

session
The active connection between a user and a COMPUTER or between two computers; a period of use of an APPLICATION or computer; one or more tracks of audio or DATA that were recorded at one time on a CD-ROM.

set up
To install a piece of hardware or software into a computer system so that it works with the system.

SETI

SETI

An enormous computing project that exploits PROCESSOR inactivity in participants' computers in order to analyze radio telescope data, the purpose being to locate extra-terrestrial sentient communication transmissions.

A downloaded SCREENSAVER uses processor idle time to analyze this data and send it back to SETI. By the end of 2003, more than a billion results from four million-plus users had been received. They still haven't found anything. SETI can be found at: http://setiathome.ssl.berkeley.edu/. *See also* DISTRIBUTED COMPUTING; PEER-TO-PEER NETWORKING.

SGML (Standard Generalized Markup Language)

A standard for defining the FORMAT of a document. SGML does not *specify* the format, but it does specify rules for TAGS. These tags can then be used to format the document. An SGML document uses a DOCUMENT TYPE DEFINITION file to define the tags within it.

SGML was launched in 1986 and has been widely used in the publishing industry. It is a very large and complex language, but has been very successful. HTML was a development using a fixed set of tags, while XML is another, simplified version of SGML. *See also* MARKUP LANGUAGE; WEB DESIGN.

shareware

software that can be obtained on a trial basis but to continue to use the program a fee must be paid to the author. Shareware programs are copyrighted. Shareware can be obtained from a variety of sources but most commonly can be downloaded from an ONLINE INFORMATION SERVICE.

sheet feeder
A device that FEEDS individual pages of paper into a printer or a scanner. The paper is drawn through by a series of friction rollers. For printing, the sheet feeder is predominantly used on LASER PRINTERS and inkjet printers.

shell
A UTILITY PROGRAM that operates as an INTERFACE between the user and an operating system that is regarded as difficult to use.

shift key
A key on a keyboard that allows the user to select an alternative range of characters such as uppercase letters, brackets, pound signs, etc. The key is identified by a white, upward facing arrow or the word "shift".

short messaging service
see SMS.

shortcut
In WINDOWS, a pointer to a PROGRAM or DATA file. Activating a shortcut is the same as opening the original file. However, deleting a shortcut does not remove the original.

shortcut key
A key or more commonly a key combination that allows the user to bypass the normal menu selection process by pressing a key or keys simultaneously. The shortcut is used for commonly-used commands such as cut and paste (Ctrl x and Ctrl v), open file (Ctrl o) or create new file (Ctrl n).

silicon

silicon
The material from which computer chips are made. It is a naturally occurring semiconductor material found in sand and clay.

Silicon Valley
An industrial area in the Santa Clara Valley in California that has a high concentration of information technology industries. It can also refer to an area with a concentration of information technology businesses.

SIM card
A SMART CARD that is inserted into GSM phones, and which contains personal telephone account information. In the mobile phone market, SIM cards are rather like an identity card. They allow you to use another phone (by swapping your card) and they can equally be set to bar such an operation for security purposes. With "pay as you go" accounts, SIM cards also have a digital money function as a payment card.

SIM stands for Subscriber Identity Module.

SIMM (Single Inline Memory Modules)
A small plug-in circuit board that contains MEMORY chips required to add more RAM to a computer. (*See also* DIMM).

simple mail transfer protocol
see SMTP.

simulation
An application based on assumptions about behavior that can be used to produce a model of real life effects.

single density
A disk storage technology that has been superseded because of the small amount of data that can be stored on the disk. The magnetic particles on the disk are relatively large compared with the much finer particles used in modern high density drives, which can typically hold about four times the amount of information.

single in-line package (SIP)
A small circuit board similar to a SIMM. Because it is more difficult to install, it is usually installed by the computer manufacturer.

single sided disk
An old type of storage disk that allows only one side to be used to read or write data. Most modern disks allow data to be written on both sides of the disk.

site license
An agreement between the authors of a computer program and a user of the program that allows the user to run the program on an agreed number of computers at one time.

site map
A hierarchical diagram of the structure of a WEBSITE showing the folders and pages on the site, starting with the HOME PAGE. Site maps help visitors to navigate around large sites. They are also used as a master diagram by web designers. *See also* PATH.

skin
A VIRTUAL façade to a GUI CONSOLE, that can be changed without affecting functionality. A skin can give a

slide show

completely different appearance to such an interface. One of the most popular examples is with MEDIA PLAYERS, where radically different designs can be adopted. There are many skins available online, but be aware that they sometimes come with additional elements that produce adverts or otherwise violate the privacy of the user.

slide show
A preset list of graphic presentations that are displayed on a screen in a predefined order. The purpose of the slide show can vary from a sales presentation to a presentation for a directors' meeting.

slot
see EXPANSION SLOT.

small cap *or* small capital
A capital letter that is smaller than a normal capital. The cross-references in this book are in SMALL CAPS, while this is the NORMAL CAPITAL.

small computer system interface
see SCSI.

smart card
A credit card (or similar) with a built-in PROCESSOR and MEMORY, used primarily for identification. When inserted into a READER, it transfers DATA to and from a central computer. Versions can be used as identity cards, credit cards, or payment cards, pre-loaded with DIGITAL MONEY and used until the balance is zero. *See also* SIM CARD.

software

smart terminal
In a NETWORK of computers, a smart terminal is one that has its own processor and secondary storage. In a network, terminals do not need to be smart, they can be DUMB TERMINALS, in which case they have no processing power or storage other than that of the network server.

SMS (Short Messaging Service)
A service offered by mobile phone NETWORK providers, enabling the user of a mobile phone to key-in text and send it to another phone user. Because the DISPLAY is so small, such messages have developed a language all of their own, including the use of EMOTICONS.

SMTP (Simple Mail Transfer Protocol)
An EMAIL standard and one of the most popular email PROTOCOLS. The main function of SMTP is to specify how messages are stored on a mail SERVER, and how mail servers collaborate to deliver a message to a recipient.

snail mail
The term sometimes used to describe the postal service as opposed to ELECTRONIC MAIL.

soft
A term used to describe a hyphen or PAGE BREAK inserted by a word processing, page layout or spreadsheet program, as opposed to a HARD command inserted by the user.

software
Any program that is loaded into a computer's internal memory and that tells the computer what function to perform. Software is also known as programs or applications.

software engineer

software engineer
Someone who designs and writes PROGRAMS for SYSTEM software, e.g. operating systems, network systems. Also, programmers who create commercial software, whatever the level. *See also* DEVELOPER; PROGRAMMER.

software license
An agreement between the user of a program and its author that gives the user the right to use one copy of it. The user pays a fee for this facility. When payment has been made for the program, the user often considers that he or she has paid for it outright, but this is not the case. The user has paid for a license to use the software and has not bought it.

software piracy
The illegal, unauthorized copying of software. Software piracy is common and costs software publishers vast amounts of money.

software publisher
The company that writes, markets, sells and distributes a computer program. Major software publishers are Microsoft, Lotus, Word Perfect.

sort
A command that organizes data into a particular order. The order can be alphabetical or numeric and can be ascending (from A to Z or 1 to 10) or descending (from Z to A or 10 to 1). A sort command is available in a wide range of applications.

sort key
in a DATABASE MANAGEMENT PROGRAM the sort key is the

FIELD name by which a SORT is to be conducted. For example, in a database of stock items the sort key could be by stock name or by stock code.

sort order

The way in which a sort places data. The most common sort order is to use the ASCII character set. This is a set of 128 characters of the alphabet (upper and lower case) and numbers plus other characters such as ",. } { ( )".

sound board

An add-on board for PERSONAL COMPUTERS that gives digital sound capabilities to a computer. MACINTOSH computers have stereo sound facilities built into the system so no added board is required.

source

The file or disk from which information or data is taken by the processor. Once the processor has performed a task the data or information is sent to its destination disk or file.

source code

The instructions that a programmer creates when writing a PROGRAM. It has to be translated or compiled into MACHINE CODE before the computer can run the program.

spam

The term given to junk mail in email transmissions. It can be a significant problem for email recipients and newsgroups but there are now sites that fight the spread of useless information.

spam filter

spam filter
SOFTWARE installed in the user's machine or in the ISP mail server, which diverts spam to a waste basket.. Spam filtering can be configured to trap messages based on a variety of criteria, including sender's EMAIL address, specific words in the subject or message body, or by the type of ATTACHMENT. Modern filters use AI to analyze message content and so increase accuracy.

SPARC (Scalar Processor ARChitecture)
A processor chip design by Sun Microsystems for computers that are used for CAD design work or other high power requirements.

special interest group
A group of like-minded users who regularly get together to discuss their chosen topic online on an INTERNET connection.

speech recognition
The ability to recognize a person by the unique characteristics of their spoken voice, for security purposes. While this is not the same as VOICE RECOGNITION, like the latter, the user has to "train" the system to understand their speech pattern. *See* BIOMETRICS.

speech synthesis
The ability to produce sound that resembles human speech, used primarily to turn text into spoken words for the visually impaired. Speech synthesis performs REAL TIME conversion, but does not create perfect human speech – the output is very intelligible, but somewhat

spell checker

A UTILITY PROGRAM or part of a larger application that individually checks each word in a document against a dictionary file. The spell checker can show the correct spelling of a word and a list of alternatives if it cannot recognize a word in the text. The chosen version is then inserted into the document.

spider software

A PROGRAM that travels around the Internet looking for recently released WEBSITES. These programs are used by SEARCH ENGINES, although a number of user-driven spiders can be found on SHAREWARE sites. When a DEVELOPER registers a site with a search engine, the engine often sends a spider to the site to produce data for the search engine's database.

spike

A surge of electricity that at best causes a system CRASH or at worst can burn out components inside the computer. A device to protect against power surges can be bought and placed between the mains supply and the computer.

split screen

A facility offered by some word processing and spreadsheet programs that allows the screen to be divided in to two or four panels so that different parts of a document can be viewed at one time. This facilitates editing processes such as copying and pasting from one part of a document to another.

spooler

spooler

A UTILITY PROGRAM that is used to facilitate printing. When the processor is sending information direct to the printer it must wait for the printer to deal with the output. Since the printer is significantly slower, the processor is not being used effectively. The processor can alternatively send the output to a spooler, which saves all the printing commands. The spooler saves the commands faster than the printer can process them so the processor is free to perform other tasks while the spooler communicates with the printer at the speed of the printer.

spreadsheet

A program that creates an on-screen worksheet, which is a series of ROWS and COLUMNS of CELLS into which values, text and formulae can be placed. The spreadsheet is recalculated whenever a change to a cell's value or formula is made. The original spreadsheet (VisiCalc) was created in 1978 for use on an Apple II computer. Since then spreadsheets have become more and more sophisticated with database management, analytical graphics, statistical analysis and many more functions available. One of the main uses of spreadsheets is WHAT IF ANALYSIS. By creating a model of a business or economy, many variables can be input in turn to assess the effect of changes in values on the economy or business.

spyware

SOFTWARE that secretly gathers information on a user through the user's Internet connection. When this is for marketing purposes, such software is known as *adware*. Spyware is often bundled as a hidden

SSL (Secure Sockets Layer)

component of FREEWARE or SHAREWARE programs. Once installed, it monitors user activity on the Internet and transmits that information elsewhere, including such things as EMAIL addresses and even passwords and credit card numbers. A common way to unwittingly install spyware is through file-swapping products. Indeed, some of these won't actually let you be a subscriber unless you allow spyware to be installed.

In addition to invading privacy, spyware can cause a SYSTEM to become unstable, leading to crashes, as well as using up BANDWIDTH. They can monitor keystrokes, scan files, install additional pernicious software, read cookies, change the BROWSER settings, and send all this information back to the originator, who might even sell the DATA on to a third party.

Regular maintenance of a system is therefore a necessity, and the use of an *anti-spyware* APPLICATION is highly recommended. It must be said, however, that some of these products are themselves intrusive and destabilizing. *See also* COOKIE; FILE SHARING

SQL
see STRUCTURED QUERY LANGUAGE.

SRAM (Static Random Access Memory)
A fast but relatively expensive MEMORY that is used to create CACHES. Information put into SRAM is held there as long as the computer power is switched on. Information from SRAM can be accessed very quickly by the processor.

SSL (Secure Sockets Layer)
The most widely used security PROTOCOL on the

stand-alone

WORLDWIDE WEB. Originally developed by NETSCAPE, it is a flexible protocol using encryption schemes ranging from domestic use, to those used for secret government data. *See also* DIGITAL MONEY.

stand-alone

A term applied to a computer system that is self-contained and has only the hardware and software required by the user.

standard

A predefined set of guidelines that is set by the industry's manufacturers to determine the type of INTERFACE between a PERIPHERAL DEVICE and the computer and the way the device communicates with the processor.

standard generalized markup language
see SGML.

standard mode

An operating mode for MICROSOFT WINDOWS that speeds up the operation of Windows applications.

star dot star

The colloquial name given to the WILDCARD search in DOS and WINDOWS. The use of *.* finds all files because the asterisk can represent any set of characters.

star network

A representation of a NETWORK where the network SERVER is located in a central position and the user stations are connected around this central point. The terminals have no connection to one another, only to the server.

start bit
The initial BIT sent in SERIAL COMMUNICATIONS that indicates to the receiving computer that the BYTE of data is about to be sent.

start-up disk
A disk that contains the operating system code required to start the computer. The start-up disk is usually a hard disk, but can be a floppy. Having a floppy disk as a start-up disk is very useful, especially if something happens to the hard disk that makes it unreadable.

start-up screen
A Macintosh graphics file that, when placed in the START-UP DISK, will be displayed on start-up. Any picture can be used.

static HTML
coding that displays a WEB PAGE that never changes, unless the SOURCE CODE is changed. A user only gets whatever information is contained in the code. In contrast, a DYNAMIC WEB PAGE contains content that a user can interact with.

stationery document
see STYLESHEET.

stop bit
The final BIT sent in SERIAL COMMUNICATIONS, which indicates to the receiving computer that the BYTE of data has been sent.

storage
The retention of programs and data in a computer

streaming

in such a way as to allow the computer processor to access the information when required. The primary storage is the RAM and ROM, and the SECONDARY STORAGE is a device such as an optical or magnetic disk drive.

streaming

Technology that allows an INTERNET user to view video or listen to audio at the same time as the data is being accessed. A MEDIA PLAYER with a BUFFER is required. This is how Internet radio works.

street price

The price at which a computer or other hardware can be bought, as compared with the official retail price set by the manufacturer. The street price is usually below the recommended price since the resellers discount the goods in order to boost or maintain their sales volumes.

string

A series of characters that can be used as a basis for a search. For example, the search string "help" will bring up all occurrences of the word or part of a word "help".

structured programming language

A computer programming language that encourages the programmer to think logically about the purpose of the program and to avoid the use of the GOTO statement (which can result in a messy unreadable program). The use of named procedures and branch control structures is encouraged. Examples of structured programming languages are C, PASCAL and ADA.

structured query language (SQL)
A set of commands used to assist users in obtaining information from a database. SQL has 30 commands and is thus relatively easy to learn and use. SQL can be used for querying databases in both personal computers and mainframe computers.

style sheet
A file that has been saved with all the FORMATTING required for a particular task. The style sheet has all the required fonts, paragraph indents, font sizes and margins. Style sheets or stationery documents can be created for many documents, such as standard letters, news sheets, promotional fliers, monthly reports, etc.

stylus
A device resembling a pen (with no ink) that is used as an INPUT DEVICE on a GRAPHICS TABLET, screen or PERSONAL DIGITAL ASSISTANT.

subdirectory
A DIRECTORY within a directory. For example, a main directory may be used to list correspondence that may be grouped into two different areas – letters and memos. The two subdirectories of the main directory would therefore be letters and memos. Letters may then have its own subdirectories for different categories.

submenu
A secondary MENU that appears as a set of OPTIONS associated with an option chosen in the main menu. In a GRAPHICAL USER INTERFACE environment using drop down menus, the submenu appears to the side of the main menu choices.

subroutine

subroutine
see ROUTINE.

subscript
Text that is printed slightly smaller and below the main body of text. The numbers in this chemical formula are in subscript: H_2SO_4

suite
A collection of several programs that fit together to provide a comprehensive set of tools that a business person may use. It should include a word processing program, a spreadsheet, an organizer, a database, a communications program and a presentation program.

super computer
A computer designed to execute very complex calculations at very high speeds. The type of problems that super computers are good at solving include weather forecasting, global warming analysis and economic analysis.

super VGA
A GRAPHICS display STANDARD that can display from 800 pixels by 600 vertical lines to 1024 pixels by 768 lines with 256 colors.

superscript
Text that is printed slightly smaller and above the main body of text. The numbers in the following are in superscript: $Y = X^2 + Z^3$

surfing
To move around the INTERNET, following up items of

interest. Surfing has become a favorite hobby for many Internet users as you can start virtually anywhere on the web and go virtually anywhere else. The term specifically refers to an organic approach, where an initial enquiry leads to other subjects being followed and then a jump to a different path of enquiry, all depending on what catches your eye.

surge protector
A device placed between a computer and the mains power supply to protect the computer from momentary increases in the voltage of the power supply.

SVG
see SCALABLE VECTOR GRAPHICS.

SVGA
see SUPER VGA.

swap file
A file used when a computer's RAM is not large enough to store the full program. A swap file is held on the hard disk, and the computer processor moves information between the RAM and the swap file as required.

symmetric digital subscriber line
see SDSL.

symmetric key encryption
ENCRYPTION where the same key is used to encrypt and decrypt the text that is to be sent, requiring the sender and the receiver to exchange the key beforehand. This exchange has to be made over a *secure channel*. The key

synchronous

used for symmetric key encryption is often known as a *secret key*. Symmetric key encryption algorithms are generally more efficient than those used in a PUBLIC KEY ENCRYPTION SYSTEM. The latter, however, is often used in order to exchange the secret keys. *See also* DIGITAL CERTIFICATE.

synchronous

A term used to describe a method of communication that is synchronized with electronic signals produced by a computer. A data BIT is sent with every tick of the computer. (*See also* PARALLEL PORT.)

syntax

The set of rules that govern the way in which a command or statement is given to a computer so that it recognizes the command and proceeds accordingly.

syntax error

An error resulting from the incorrect spelling of a command or in the way the commands are entered. For example, DOS commands must be entered in strict order of command first, then parameters and then switches.

SYS-OP (system operator)

The person who is in charge of a BULLETIN BOARD or an area in an ONLINE INFORMATION SERVICE. The SYSOP is responsible for helping users and ensuring that the rules of the bulletin board are maintained.

system date

The date that is held in a computer's internal memory. This memory is not subject to loss when the computer's power is switched off as it is protected by a battery backup.

system software

system disk
A disk containing the operating system and all related files. The system disk can be a floppy or a hard disk.

system error
An error that occurs at the SYSTEM level of operation of a computer, as opposed to a user-generated error. System errors may be caused by bad programming.

system file
A MACHINE LANGUAGE file that is part of the OPERATING SYSTEM or other control program. File extension SYS.

system or computer system
All the necessary hardware and software required in an installation, all of which is interconnected and set up to work together (central processing unit, disk drives, monitor, printer, keyboard, and so on).

system program
see ROM.

system prompt
An indicator to show that the OPERATING SYSTEM is ready to accept a command. The system prompt is seen in command line operating systems as opposed to GRAPHICAL USER INTERFACE systems. In DOS the system prompt is C> where **c** represents the current disk drive.

system software
The group of codes that the computer requires to start up. It includes the OPERATING SYSTEM, which controls all the major functions of the computer.

system tray or systray

system tray *or* **systray**
located in the WINDOWS taskbar and containing icons for fast access to SYSTEM functions such as fax, printer, modem, volume, etc.

system unit
The primary computer equipment. Housed in a desktop or tower cabinet, it contains such components as the MOTHERBOARD, CPU, RAM and ROM chips, hard and floppy disks and several INPUT/OUTPUT ports.

T

tab key
In a text-editing program a key that is used to move text to the right by a fixed or preset number of spaces. The tab key can be used to indent the first line in a paragraph or to create a table of columns. The number of spaces that the text moves to the right is determined by the TAB STOPS. These can be set at any value. The tab key is also used to move the CURSOR between on-screen command OPTIONS.

tab stop
The point where the cursor stops when the tab key is pressed. Normally the tabs are preset at half an inch but can be altered to any value. There are normally four types of tab stops: left tab stop aligns the text to the left side of the tab stop; right tab stop aligns itself to the right of the tab stop; center tab stop aligns the text centrally under the tab stop; decimal tab stop aligns the decimal point of a number under the tab stop.

table
Text that is arranged in rows and columns in order to display information. A table is also the basic structure for storage of data in DATABASE MANAGEMENT PROGRAMS. Rows correspond to records, and columns correspond to fields of data.

table of contents (TOC)
A list of the main items in a WEBSITE. Items in a table of contents are usually HYPERTEXT, i.e. they LINK to other

tag

locations within the site for ease of NAVIGATION. The HOME PAGE often serves as a table of contents. In many INTERNET PUBLISHING software applications, the TOC is actually a UTILITY that is automatically generated and amends itself when necessary. *See* WEB AUTHORING.

Also, a part of the specifications of a recorded OPTICAL DISK, giving the number of tracks, their starting locations, total length of DATA on the disc, and identification of type of disc. *See* CD BURNING; OPTICAL DISK.

tag

A MARKUP LANGUAGE command in a DOCUMENT that specifies how the document should be formatted. *See* HTML, XML.

Also, a name assigned to a data structure, such as a FIELD; the key field in a RECORD.

tagged image file format
see TIFF.

tape

A thin strip of plastic, coated with a magnetic recording material, that is normally held in a plastic case. It is used principally as a backup storage medium. It is not used for secondary storage because of the relatively long access time to retrieve data that is a long way into the tape. Data is held sequentially on the tape and since the tape is held on reels the last data to be saved to the tape is at the end of the reel. If the user wants to access the data at the end of the reel the tape drive must spin the reels from the start to the end of the tape. This could take several minutes thus precluding the tape drive as anything but backup storage.

telecommunications

tape drive
DEVICE that reads data from and writes it to a tape. Tape drives have capacities of anything from a few hundred kilobytes to several gigabytes. Fast tape drives can transfer as much as 20Mb per second.

target
what a HYPERLINK points to. The hyperlink is written as a text description of the PATH to the file that will be activated by using the LINK. The link is created by using an HTML TAG.

Also, generally, the destination point of any path is the target. The start point is the SOURCE or ROOT.

tb, tbyte
see TERABYTE.

TCP / IP (Transmission Control Protocol or Internet Protocol)
A cross-platform communications protocol which allows computers with different operating systems to communicate.

technical support
The provision by hardware or software manufacturers of information and trouble-shooting advice, which is available for registered users, usually by email or telephone.

telecommunications
The use of the telephone systems, either land lines or satellite, to transmit information (voice, video or computer data).

telecommute

telecommute
To work from a home base rather than commute to the office. Telecommuting has been made possible by the efficiency of the telephone systems. An employee can perform tasks at home and send results to the office computer by using a MODEM. In addition, messages can be transmitted to the employee at home through an ELECTRONIC MAIL system. People who work at home in this way are sometimes called *teleworkers*.

teleworker
see TELECOMMUTE.

Telnet
The main Internet protocol for creating a connection to other remote computers and Internet locations worldwide. Examples include EWAN (Windows) and NCSA Telnet (Macintosh).

template
A document that is prewritten and formatted and ready for final editing or adjustment before printing.

temporary file
A FILE created by an APPLICATION for its own purposes. Temporary files are used to store interim DATA and are then deleted when the application is closed. The application is responsible for deleting its own temporary files, but the files often remain on-disk. Temporary files generally use a TMP file extension and are often known as TEMP files. A fine collection can usually be found in the TEMP folder of the Windows directory.

tera (T)
A prefix representing one trillion (1012).

terabyte (Tb, tbyte)
A measurement of MEMORY capacity that is approximately equal to one trillion BYTES. The actual number is 1,099,511,627,776 bytes.

terminal
An INPUT/OUTPUT device consisting of a monitor, keyboard and connection to a central server. A terminal can be a DUMB TERMINAL, which has no processor or secondary storage, or a SMART TERMINAL, which has these facilities and can thus operate on its own as well as operate as part of the NETWORK.

terminal emulation
A procedure whereby a TERMINAL or PERSONAL COMPUTER acts like another in order that communications can take place between computers.

text alignment
The JUSTIFICATION of text in a word processing or page layout document. Text is aligned with reference to the right and left margins of the page. Text can be lined up with the right margin (unusual), the left margin (most common) the center of the page (for headings) or can be fully justified (spread out so that the text reaches both the left and right margins).

text chart
In business presentations a slide presentation that contains no graphics. The slide consists only of text, e.g. showing a menu list of items.

text editor

text editor
A basic word processing program that is used mainly for writing computer programs and batch files. It has very limited facilities for formatting and printing.

text file
A file that contains only ASCII characters. This file type is used mainly for transfer of information between different programs or computers. The file does not contain any formatting codes that could indicate bold or italic text or differing fonts or font sizes. The use of text files is diminishing as many programs have automated FILE TRANSFER procedures to allow one program to read a file created in another program.

text graphics file
Most commonly for the web, a GIF or JPEG file containing only text, used in WEB DESIGN when FONT INCOMPATIBILITY seems likely. Because the text is part of a GRAPHICS FILE, it displays as a graphic image and is therefore stable. It is used for items like headings.

text message
A typed piece of text that can be sent by a cellular phone. The popular name for messages sent by SMS (SHORT MESSAGING SERVICE).

text to speech (TTS)
see SPEECH SYNTHESIS.

text wrap
see WRAP AROUND TYPE.

texture mapping

in computer GRAPHICS, the digital representation of the surface of an object, whether a brick wall, or wood grain. One method of texture mapping is to create a 2-D bitmapped image of the texture. Once this has been defined, it can be wrapped around any 3-D object. Alternatively, one can compute the texture entirely via mathematics, which can create more precise textures. *See also* AGP; BITMAP; CGI; RENDER.

thermal printer

A printer that uses heat to form an image on special paper. The thermal heads heat the paper, which has a wax-type coating causing a discoloration that results in print. Some fax machines use this type of printing device.

thesaurus

A book or file that lists alternative meanings for words, i.e. synonyms. Most word processing programs now include an electronic thesaurus that displays a list of synonyms for each word selected. Once the new word has been chosen, the program will replace the old word with the new.

third generation

An era in computing around the mid-1960s when the transistor was replaced by INTEGRATED CIRCUITS and disk storage and ONLINE terminals were introduced.

thread

A link between an article in a newsgroup and any responses to that article.

three-dimensional spreadsheet

throughput

A SPREADSHEET program that consists of several layers of related pages or worksheets. For example, if a company has four stores, a worksheet can be created for each store to show its income and expenditure. In order to produce a consolidation of the results of the four stores a fifth worksheet is created that calculates the sum of the figures for each store.

throughput

A measure of a computer's overall speed of performance as opposed to the speed of a particular element of the computer or system. The slowest component will effectively determine the performance of the computer.

tick

A single beat of the MICROCHIP that determines the number of instructions that a chip can process. Normally a chip can process one instruction per tick.

TIFF (Tagged Image File Format)

A STANDARD relating to graphic images. A TIFF file contains a series of dots (*see* BITMAP) that makes up the image. The dots can be printed, stored on a disk or displayed on a monitor.

tile

To set windows in a side-by-side fashion on the desktop. Tiling windows shrinks the size of the windows so that more can be seen on the screen. Windows can be tiled or shown as CASCADING WINDOWS.

time sharing

A technique for sharing resources in a MULTI-USER

system. Users do not notice that they are sharing the system resources. If the system does become overloaded with users, they will notice a decline in the operating speed.

Title bar

A shaded bar containing the name of the file that is found at the top of an on screen window in GRAPHICAL USER INTERFACE systems. The title bar is shaded when the WINDOW is active.

TOC

see TABLE OF CONTENTS.

toggle

A key OPTION that allows switching back and forth between states of operation, i.e. the FUNCTION is switched on and off. The caps lock key is a toggle key that alternatively switches to uppercase mode and back to lowercase mode each time the key is pressed.

token

in networks, a token is a series of BITS that travels around a TOKEN-RING NETWORK and can be captured by users. The token acts like a ticket, enabling its owner to send a message across the network. As there is only one token for each network, there is no possibility that two computers will attempt to do the same thing at the same time.

token passing

A PROTOCOL in which tokens move around a NETWORK. When a NODE wants to send a message over the network

token ring network

it has to obtain a free token. The node that controls the token controls the network until the message has been passed and acknowledged.

token ring network

A LOCAL AREA NETWORK that uses token passing technology as the basis for communications.

toner

powdered ink that is electrically charged and is used in laser printers and photocopying machines. The toner is applied to a charged drum and fused to the paper with a heating element.

tool

A software enhancement or system maintenance UTILITY designed for use by programmers; a program that helps in the processing of DATA, e.g. report tools; an on-screen FUNCTION in a GRAPHICS program; a MENU function in an APPLICATION that links to options, preferences and/or other utilities.

toolbar

A strip of buttons that appears at the top of the screen that are used to select commands without using menus. The tool bars can be edited so that the user can choose the buttons that are most appropriate to the tasks that are being undertaken. Tool bars are commonly used in word processing and other software packages.

toolbox

A set of prewritten programs or routines used by programmers for incorporation into larger programs.

tower system

This saves time and ensures that there is consistent implementation of the toolbox routines, such as printing.

toolkit
A set of SOFTWARE utilities to help develop and maintain applications, data and systems. *See also* TOOL.

top down programming
A method of designing programs. It starts with a basic statement of the program's main objectives, which is then divided into sub-objectives, and so on. The sub-objectives or subcategories are of a type that can be programmed easily. C and PASCAL are STRUCTURED PROGRAMMING LANGUAGES that lend themselves to top down programming.

topology
A LOCAL AREA NETWORK layout. Topologies can be centralized or decentralized. A centralized network is like a star and a decentralized network is like a ring.

touch sensitive display
A type of screen with a pressure sensitive panel in front of the screen. The panel is effectively lined up with the display options, which are selected by pressing the panel at the correct place. This type of screen technology is used for public information access rather than in business.

tower system
of style of computer system in which the electronics, disk drives, expansions cards, etc, are contained in a box resembling a tower that usually sits on the floor beside

Tpi

the user's desk. The VDU and keyboard sit on the desk. (*See also* MINI TOWER.)

Tpi
see TRACKS PER INCH.

track
one of a number of concentric circles on a floppy or hard disk. The track is encoded on the disk during FORMATTING and is a particular area on the disk for data storage.

trackball
An INPUT DEVICE that is similar to a mouse that is turned upside down. Instead of moving the mouse over the desk to move the ball, the ball is moved within a static unit that may be embedded in the case of a LAPTOP COMPUTER.

trackpad
An INPUT DEVICE that is a development of the trackball. It consists of a square pad embedded in the case of a LAPTOP COMPUTER, and movement of the finger over the pad moves the cursor on the screen.

tracks per inch (tpi)
A measure of the density of data storage on floppy disks, higher figures representing a greater capacity for data.

tractor feed
A mechanism, similar to PIN FEED, that is used in dot matrix printers to push the paper past the print head. The mechanism has sprockets that engage in pre-punched perforations at the edges of the paper.

TrueType

traffic
A general term referring to the overall level of DATA transmission in a NETWORK at a given moment. It can also refer to specific transactions, messages, or records.

transfer
To move information from disk to memory and vice versa.

translate
To change a file that has been saved in one file format to another so that the file can be opened in a different program.

tree structure
A way of organizing directories on a disk that shows the core or main directory at the top with the various subdirectories and sub-subdirectories shown like the branches of a tree extending downwards and outwards.

trojan horse
A program that appears to perform a valid function but, in fact, contains hidden codes that can cause damage to the system that runs the program. It does not replicate itself or infect other files as a VIRUS does.

troubleshoot
To investigate the reason for a particular occurrence or malfunction in a computer system. Very often a failure is caused, not by a major problem, but a small error that can be rectified quite easily.

TrueType
A font technology that rivals Postscript and displays on-screen

fonts exactly as the printer prints them out. The fonts are SCALABLE and so, no matter which font size is chosen, the screen display and the printer will be the same. TrueType fonts do not require any special printer processors, unlike Postscript fonts, to enable them to be printed, and so the TrueType document is portable between systems.

truncate
To cut off part of an entry (a number or character string) either to ensure that it fits a predefined space or to reduce the number of characters for easier processing.

TTS (Text To Speech)
see SPEECH SYNTHESIS.

tutorial
A process of instructions that guides the user through a series of steps designed to show the features of a program such as a word processor, database or spreadsheet.

Twain
The interface STANDARD for scanners. Nearly all SCANNERS come with a TWAIN driver, although not all scanner software is TWAIN-compatible.

type ahead buffer
A memory BUFFER that stores the characters being typed on the keyboard so that they can be processed by the RAM when the processor is free.

type style
refers to the WEIGHT of type or the slope of the type as

typeface

opposed to the size of the type or the typeface. The weight of type refers to how **bold** the type appears and the slope of type refers to whether *italic style* is chosen.

typeface

A set of characters sharing a unique design, such as Courier or Times. Typefaces can be SERIF or SANS SERIF.

U

UDF (Universal Disk Format)
A file system for CD-ROMs and other optical media that allows one operating system to read and write data that was created by another operating system. DVDs, CD-R and CD-RW disks use UDF. *See also* DUAL-PLATFORM DISK; CD BURNING.

ultra DMA
An enhanced version of the IDE INTERFACE, that transfers data at 33, 66 or 100 Mbps.

UML (Unified Modeling Language)
A general-purpose LANGUAGE for specifying complex software, especially large, OBJECT-oriented projects.

undelete program
A UTILITY PROGRAM that is used to restore files that have been deleted from a disk, possibly by accident. The recovery (*see* RECOVER) of the file depends on there having been no other data written onto the disk since the file was deleted as this would affect the storage areas.

underline
A command used to highlight text by placing a line under the selected word or portion of text. Double underline can also be used in some word processing packages.

undo
A command available in programs that reverses the effect

of the previous command given. It allows the user to cancel the effect of a command that has had an unforeseen or disastrous effect.

undocumented
features of programs that have not been documented in the program manual.

unencode
A program used to convert a file into an ASCII file so that it can be transmitted as a text message.

unformatted
A term indicating that an item of MAGNETIC MEDIA requires FORMATTING prior to being put into operation.

Unicode
A cross-platform character encoding standard developed with the aim of providing a universal way of encoding all of the characters of the world's main languages, creating a universal character set. Unique character codes are assigned to letters and symbols. There is room for over 65,000 distinct Unicode characters. It was developed by the Unicode Consortium, see www.unicode.org, a non-profit-making organisation developed to promote this standard. The aim is to allow interchange and display of any script, of any language, by any computer with any operating system.

uniform resource locator
see URL.

uninterruptible power supply (UPS)
A power supply that switches to an alternative power

universal serial bus

source, such as a battery, in the event of the main supply crashing. The alternative will probably have a short life but will be long enough to allow proper shutdown to take place, thus preserving data.

universal serial bus
see USB.

UNIX
An OPERATING SYSTEM suitable for a wide range of computers from MAINFRAMES to PERSONAL COMPUTERS. It is suited to MULTIUSER situations and can handle MULTITASKING.

unprotected software
Software that can be copied from the original program disks on to other floppy disks or onto a hard disk. Retaining a copy of a program disk is sensible in case of damage to the original.

update
To revise the contents of a file, usually a database file, so that the contents reflect the correct and current state.

upgrade
To purchase the most recent version of software released by the author or to purchase a new hardware update, such as a new computer system.

upload
To copy a file from your computer to another computer connected through the telecommunication system. (*See also* DOWNLOAD.)

uppercase
Type in capital letters as opposed to lower case.
THESE ARE UPPERCASE CHARACTERS
These are lowercase characters

upstream
Transmission from an end user to a provider. An upstream transmission can be a signal transmitted from a WORKSTATION to a SERVER across a NETWORK, or a request being sent from a customer to a cable service provider. Contrast with DOWNSTREAM.

upward compatibility
The ability of an application program to run under a more advanced computer or operating system than it was originally designed for.

URL (Uniform Response Locator)
Identifies the location of files on servers.

USB (Universal Serial Bus)
An external BUS standard that acts as a HARDWARE interface for PERIPHERALS. A USB PORT can connect tens of such devices, such as mice, modems, keyboards and printers via a HUB. USB also supports PLUG AND PLAY and HOT SWAPPING. USB first appeared on MACINTOSH computers and has since spread in use. USB 2.0 has dramatically increased speeds and capacities. USB plugs and sockets are either of type A or B, depending on the nature of the DEVICE. *See also* HANDHELDS.

USB hub
A DEVICE that attaches to the computer's USB PORT and which increases the number of USB ports available. As one socket

Usenet

can provide up to 127 connections, there is no practical limit to the number of sockets in a hub, but they generally come in denominations of four or eight A-type sockets.

Usenet
A collection of all the NEWSGROUPS.

user
The person who is operating the computer.

user group
A gathering of people with similar objectives who communicate through computers.

user interface
A means by which the user communicates with the computer. The different user INTERFACEs include a GRAPHICS USER INTERFACE, in which the user communicates through MENUs and ICONs, and the command line interface in which the user has to type the appropriate command at a PROMPT.

user-defined
A selection of preferences chosen by the user of a computer.

user-friendly
jargon for a system that is easy to learn and operate. Computers using GRAPHICAL USER INTERFACE are user-friendly.

utility
A program that helps the user to obtain the most benefit from a computer system by performing routine tasks, e.g. copying data from one file to another. *See also* DESK ACCESSORY.

V

V42 bis
A data compression and error correction STANDARD used for communications between MODEMS.

vaccine
A UTILITY designed to prevent a computer VIRUS from attacking a system.

value
A numeric CELL entry in a SPREADSHEET program. A value can be a constant that is entered directly into a cell or it can be the product of a formula.

vaporware
Software under development that is marketed in advance of its release. Often the release is delayed because of technical problems but the marketing goes on, creating the impression that the software does not exist.

VDT (Video Display Terminal)
see VDU.

VDU (Visual Display Unit) or monitor or screen or video display
A device that incorporates a cathode-ray tube and produces a picture of computer input or output. The display is created by firing a series of rays at a phosphorus-coated screen. The screen colors are created by mixing red, green and blue. There is some

vector font

concern that the electromagnetic radiation given out by VDUs may be hazardous. They emit X-rays, ultraviolet radiation, electrostatic discharge and electromagnetic fields.

vector font
see SCALABLE FONT.

vector graphics
A technique for representing an image as points, lines and geometric shapes. Vector graphics tend to take up less MEMORY than a BITMAP, as the image is a representation of a mathematical formula, rather than a collection of dots. CAD and DRAW PROGRAMS utilize vector graphics.

FONTS represented as vectors (e.g. POSTSCRIPT) are known variously as VECTOR FONTS, SCALABLE FONTS, OBJECT-ORIENTED FONTS, and OUTLINE FONTS. Most OUTPUT DEVICES can only handle bitmapped images, which means that vector graphics objects must be translated into bitmaps before being output. PostScript printers, for example, have a RASTER IMAGE PROCESSOR that performs the translation.

Vector graphics are also known as OBJECT-ORIENTED GRAPHICS. *See also* PAINT PROGRAM.

verify
A computer procedure that ensures that an operation was completed correctly.

Veronica
A SEARCH ENGINE specialized for gopher sites, just as ARCHIE is specialized for FTP sites. Veronica uses a

video display

SPIDER program to create an index of the files on all Gopher servers. You can then search the Veronica system.

version number
The number assigned to a version or release of a program. Each time the author revises the program the version number is amended. Minor changes are indicated with a change in the decimal point while major changes are reflected in the main number.

VESA (Video Electronics Standards Association)
A grouping of manufacturers who have devised STANDARDS to ensure that computers and VDUs are compatible.

video adapter
The electronic card that generates the graphic output that is displayed on a VDU.

video card
see VIDEO ADAPTER.

video disk
An optical storage device used for pictures, movies and sound. The disk has a high storage capacity holding up to two hours of TV pictures. Video disks can be used for interactive video when the disk is placed under the control of a computer.

video display
see VDU

video RAM

video RAM
see VRAM.

view
An on-screen display of the contents of a file or part of a file. In DATABASE MANAGEMENT PROGRAMS a view can be generated to look at a selection of records. The selection depends on the criteria specified in a QUERY command.

virtual
A feature or state that is simulated, or not real. The antonym of PHYSICAL. One of the first uses of the term was for VIRTUAL MEMORY, where RAM is temporarily saved to HARD DISK and swapped back and forth as needed – thus, memory is simulated on disk.

virtual community
NETWORK users who are linked by a subject of mutual interest. There are a variety of methods of linking up such communities, including BULLETIN BOARD SERVICES, FORUMS, CHAT ROOMS, and BLOGS.

virtual drive
Part of a computer's internal memory that is defined to act like a DISK DRIVE. Data can be stored temporarily in the virtual drive and accessed very quickly by the main processor.

virtual machine
A computerized version of a computer that acts as if the computer was real and can run applications.

virtual memory (VM)
The use of disk drive storage to extend the RAM of a

computer. Because the processor treats virtual memory like RAM, the use of VM slows down the computer processing speed.

virtual private network
see VPN.

virtual reality
A computer-generated environment that allows the user to experience various aspects of life without the travel or the danger that may be associated with the activities. A head-mounted display and sensor glove are used to create the effect.

virtual reality modeling language
see VRML.

virus
A program that is designed to cause damage to systems that the virus infects. A virus program can copy itself from file to file and disk to disk and can therefore spread quickly through a computer system. It can also move between computers through the use of infected disks and also through telecommunication systems.

visual display unit
see VDU.

visual programming
Working with programming APPLICATIONS that have an advanced GUI, with TOOLS that allow menus, buttons and other GRAPHICS elements to be selected from a PALETTE and drawn and built on-screen, and which

voice mail

graphically display the LOGIC PATHS and associated code. *See also* PROGRAMMING; RAPID APPLICATION DEVELOPMENT.

voice mail

A system that stores voice communication on disk and can replay the message on command. Voice mail systems can be combined with telephone systems to provide computerized answer machines.

voice recognition

The conversion of speech into computer text. A DIGITAL recording of speech is matched against a dictionary of waveforms, the matches being converted into text as if the words were input at the KEYBOARD.

Speaker-dependent applications require the speaker to enunciate samples into the system in order to "tune" it to their voice. These systems are called *discrete speech systems*. *Speaker-independent* (or *continuous speech*) systems do not require tuning but, until recently, could only recognize limited vocabularies. Electronic phone operators are a case in point. Recently, great strides have been made in continuous speech systems.

Such systems are useful in instances where the user is unable to use a keyboard. Increasingly, however, voice recognition systems are being thought of as an alternative to keyboards. *See also* SPEECH SYNTHESIS; WAI

voice synthesis

see SPEECH SYNTHESIS.

voice/data switch

A switch that identifies the type of call being received over a telephone line and that routes the call to the appropriate device. Voice calls go to a telephone and fax calls to a fax machine.

volatile storage
Storage of which the contents are lost when power is removed, e.g. the RAM.

volume
A fixed area or amount of MEMORY storage on a DISK. In a partitioned disk, each partition equals a volume. Often synonymous with the storage medium itself.

volume label
A name that identifies the disk. The name is given when the disk is formatted (*see* FORMAT).

VPN (Virtual Private Network)
A NETWORK with the Internet as the medium for transporting DATA. These systems use ENCRYPTION and other security mechanisms to ensure that only authorized users can access the network and that the data cannot be intercepted.

VRAM (Video RAM)
RAM used in conjunction with a video card together to enhance the performance of video displays.

VRML (Virtual Reality Modeling Language)
Specification for displaying 3-D OBJECTS on the worldwide web. To view these files, you need a VRML BROWSER or a VRML PLUG-IN to a browser. VRML produces a 3-D space that appears on your DISPLAY screen. You can move within this space.

W

W3C
see WORLDWIDE WEB CONSORTIUM.

WAI (Web Accessibility Initiative)
An initiative of the W3C tasked to help ensure that WEBSITES are designed to accommodate people with disabilities. The guidelines that the WAI have released cover visual, aural, physical and neurological disabilities and the aspects of web design that are pertinent to these, e.g. reliance on visual elements on a page, keyboard command support, use of over-complex language or structure. Further the WAI works within the following areas in pursuit of accessibility: technology compliance; guideline development; evaluation tools development; education and outreach; research and development. The work of this crucial organization can be found at: http://www.w3.org/WAI/.

WAIS (Wide Area Information Server)
An application that is used to search the thousands of databases connected to the INTERNET for a selection of keywords.

wait state
The interval programmed into a computer during which the MICROPROCESSOR waits for the RAM to catch up. As processors are built to run at faster speeds, the memory must be designed to keep up. If this does not happen then the faster processors will be worthless.

wallpaper
An on-screen design that acts as a backdrop to the ICONS, WINDOWS, etc. GRAPHICAL USER INTERFACE computer operating systems have facilities to change the patterns through CONTROL PANELS.

WAN
see WIDE AREA NETWORK.

WAP (Wireless Application Protocol)
A PROTOCOL that allows a mobile phone user to access the INTERNET or specific NETWORK service. Introduced in 1997, WAP provides a complete environment for wireless applications and features the *Wireless Markup Language* (WML), a mini-version of HTML for small screen displays. It runs on all major WIRELESS NETWORKS and is device-independent. WML is scalable from two-line text displays to the screens found on PDAs.

warm boot
A system restart that is initiated usually because a system error has occurred during operations. A warm boot will reset the memory and reload the OPERATING SYSTEM but may not reset PERIPHERALS such as modems. A complete power shutdown and restart may be required for such operations. (*See also* BOOT).

web
Short form of WORLDWIDE WEB.

Web Accessibility Initiative
see WAI.

web authoring

web authoring

To design and create a WEBSITE in its entirety, including structure, coding, and provision of all linked matter, and, by implication, the maintenance and updating of the site.

Also, creation and editing SOFTWARE that allows WEB PAGES to be visually created, like a DESKTOP PUBLISHING PROGRAM. The software generates the HTML coding based on what the user designs graphically. The user can toggle between the graphical design and the CODE and make changes to the page in either mode. Such packages are extremely powerful and sophisticated and include complete website management tools. Well-known examples include Macromedia Dreamweaver and Microsoft FrontPage. *See also* WYSIWYG EDITOR.

web browser

see BROWSER.

web design

designing a WEBSITE. There are a number of criteria: the pages should be uncluttered, clearly declare their intent, and the material on the pages must be able to be read easily; NAVIGATION between pages must be easy, and users must be able to know where they are within the website. Also, the site should DOWNLOAD quickly and effortlessly. A lot of this comes with understanding what a user will want from the site, and what equipment they are looking at it with. ACCESSIBILITY is a subject all in itself – see WAI.

Web designers might use WEB AUTHORING software or an HTML EDITOR to create the actual pages, or they might just design the graphic "look" of the site and let a WEBMASTER do the rest.

webcast

Another aspect of web design is in obtaining LINKS with other sites, and from them to you, as well as SEARCH ENGINE optimization, and also in providing regular, competent maintenance and updating.

It's a big subject, so it is not surprising that many people elect to undertake a course of some kind. It is also not surprising that many sites fail these criteria.

See http://www.webpagesthatsuck.com/.

web font
see EMBEDDED FONT.

web page
An HTML document forming part of a WEBSITE on the WWW.

web server
A FILE SERVER that is DEDICATED to the provision of WEB PAGES across the Internet, via the HTTP.

web server error message
code that is returned from the WEB SERVER to the user's BROWSER, indicating the status of the request. Generally, this is restricted to error messages, particularly the well known "404 – Not Found" and "500 – Internal Server Error"...there are many others, formally known as *HTML return codes*. To be a 404 is slang for someone who is generally uninformed.

webcast
A broadcast audio or video transmission on the WEB, e.g. an academic lecture or a press conference. Users require a MEDIA PLAYER that can handle video or audio STREAMING.

weblog

weblog
see BLOG.

webmaster
A person who is responsible for a WEBSITE, potentially including: WEB DESIGN, site maintenance and updating, ensuring that the WEB SERVER hardware and software is running properly, replying to user feedback, monitoring traffic. *See* WEB AUTHORING.

web ring
A series of WEBSITES linked together so that the LINKS form a closed circuit – you will always navigate yourself back to where you started. Each web ring is devoted to a particular subject or has some other shared purpose. Web rings are a way of encouraging more users to visit the sites within the ring. *See also* BLOG; VIRTUAL COMMUNITY.

website
A location on the WORLDWIDE WEB, with a URL, containing a number of HTML documents, comprising a HOME PAGE, and additional pages and files in an ordered and interconnected structure, providing cohesive and coherent information on a particular subject to a visitor. Each site is owned and managed by an individual, company or organization.

weight
The relative thickness and thinness of type. Different TYPE STYLES can have different weights and within a particular style the weight can be graduated between extra light and extra bold.

what if analysis
A procedure using a SPREADSHEET to explore the effect of changes in one input into a calculation. For example, what will happen to profits if volumes of sales are increased by reducing the selling price?

white paper
Authoritative report on a topic. There are countless white papers, written by vendors, research firms and consultants, many of which are now available on the web.

WHOIS
Internet UTILITY that returns information about a DOMAIN NAME or IP ADDRESS. For a personal website, this will include the registrar and registrant's details. This is called *looking up*.

wide area network (WAN)
A computer NETWORK that connects computers over long distances using telephone lines or satellite communications. A wide area network can span the world whereas a LOCAL AREA NETWORK can cover only a few miles.

wi-fi (wireless fidelity)
certification scheme for ETHERNET devices that comply with the relevant standard.

wild card
A special character that is substituted for another character or range of characters in a search of FILENAMES. In DOS, an asterisk is a substitute for a number of characters while a question mark is a substitute for one

Win32

character. For example, a search for *ook will find book, look, shook, and so on, whereas a search for ?ook will find book and look, but not shook.

Win32

The API for 32-bit Windows OPERATING SYSTEMS, including Windows NT, 95, 98 and 2000 and XP. An APPLICATION written to Win32 can run in all operating systems except where there are system-specific features that are unavailable in the others. For example, Windows NT provides security features that are not in Windows 95/98.

Winchester

A type of HARD DISK used for data storage.

window

An on-screen frame, usually rectangular in shape, that contains the display of a file. Multiple windows can be open on a desktop at a time.

Windows (Microsoft Windows)

A comprehensive software facility that utilizes the GRAPHICAL USER INTERFACE features that were once the domain of the MACINTOSH. These include PULL-DOWN MENUS, a variety of accessories and the facility of moving text and graphics from one program to another. It is possible to run several programs at once, each within a separate window, and to move from one to the other very quickly. All applications that run within the Windows system have a common way of working with windows, dialog boxes, etc.

wireless application protocol
see WAP.

wireless network
A NETWORK where each communicating DEVICE (e.g. computer, PDA) has a transceiver and can communicate both with other devices and with the NETWORK SERVER in the normal way. Such networks are more expensive to install, and have historically had a poor security and privacy record, but are now much more effective. A recent development has been in the technologies that allow a mobile user to connect to public access networks, via HOTSPOTS. *See also* WAP.

wizard
A computerized EXPERT SYSTEM that leads the user through the sometimes complex process of creating a document such as an advertising flyer or a newsletter.

WLAN (Wireless Local Area Network)
see WIRELESS NETWORK.

word count
A feature of many programs that provides the user with a total number of words contained in a document. It is an invaluable feature of word processing programs.

word processing
A method of document preparation, storage and editing using a microcomputer/personal computer.

word wrap
A feature of word processing programs that automatically

work group

moves words down to the next line if they go beyond the right-hand margin.

work group

A small group of employees assigned to work together on a specific project. The work group can become more productive if personal computer technology is used to its best effect, i.e. if LOCAL AREA NETWORKS, ELECTRONIC MAIL, shared databases, and so on, are utilized.

workbook

A three-dimensional SPREADSHEET.

working directory

The DIRECTORY in which you are currently working. Synonymous with *current directory*. All PATHS that do not specify the ROOT DIRECTORY are assumed by the OPERATING SYSTEM to start from the working directory. *See also* RELATIVE LINK.

worksheet

A matrix of rows and columns in a SPREADSHEET program into which are entered headings, numbers and formulae.

workstation

A desktop computer in a LOCAL AREA NETWORK that serves as an access point to the network. Programs can be run from the workstation, and all network resources can be accessed.

worldwide web

A HYPERTEXT-based document retrieval system linked to the INTERNET. Each page is indexed and can be linked

write

to a related document. The worldwide web is allowing easier access to information available on the Internet.

Worldwide Web Consortium (W3C)
An international consortium of companies, founded in 1994 by Tim Berners-Lee, the original architect of the WORLDWIDE WEB, to develop STANDARDS for the web and ensure that it evolves in a unified manner. More than 400 organizations are involved, and many of the projects undertaken have produced lasting standards for fundamental technologies, e.g. CSS, HTML, URL, XML. *See also* WAI.

worm
A virus in the form of a program that makes copies of itself from one disk drive to another, or through email. It may do serious damage or compromise security.

WORM disk
A disk that is Write Once, Read Many times. Generally refers to an OPTICAL DISK, because the data is physically burnt onto their surface. CD-R and DVD-R/+R are WORM disks. *See also* CD-ROM; DVD.

wrap around type
Type that is contoured so that it surrounds a graphic item in a document. This is a feature of desktop publishing programs such as PageMaker, where it is called text wrap.

write
An operation of the CENTRAL PROCESSING UNIT that records information on to a computer's RAM. It more commonly

write/protect

refers to the recording of information on to SECONDARY STORAGE media such as disk drives.

write/protect

To protect a file or disk so that a user cannot modify or erase its data. A write/protect tab can be seen in the bottom right-hand corner of the back of a floppy disk, which, when slid down, protects the disk in this fashion.

writer

general term for any DEVICE or SOFTWARE that transmits data to a STORAGE medium, or creates or transforms a document in some way. (E.g. PDF writer; CD writer).

WYSIWYG (What You See Is What You Get)

The feature that what is seen on the screen is exactly what is replicated when the information is printed.

WYSIWYG editor

A WEB PAGE authoring and editing PROGRAM that provides a WYSIWYG (What you See Is What You Get) view of your HTML documents. Such editors have become very sophisticated - the most sophisticated offer a plethora of facilities for all aspects of WEBSITE development. *See also* WEB AUTHORING.

XYZ

x-axis
The horizontal axis of a GRAPH. The horizontal axis usually contains the categories of values being plotted. For example, creating a graph of monthly sales will require that time be plotted on the horizontal or x-axis and sales be plotted on the vertical or y-axis.

XHTML
A combination of HTML and XML, XHTML is a MARKUP LANGUAGE written in XML that enables HTML to be extended with proprietary TAGS. It ensures that layout and presentation stay constant and true to the original, regardless of platform. XHTML markup must conform to the standards defined in a HTML DTD and is also coded more rigorously than HTML. It is set to be the new standard in WEB DESIGN.

XML (eXtensible Markup Language)
Developed by the W3C, XML is a simplified form of SGML, designed to deal with some of the problems with HTML, one being that HTML is not easy to extend, or add to, for reasons of version compatibility. Another problem with HTML is that it can't differentiate the actual content of a page (i.e. it doesn't understand what the content actually is).

XML defines DATA elements on a web page, using a similar TAG structure to HTML. Whereas HTML defines how elements are displayed, XML defines what those elements contain. Where HTML has a catalog of

xmodem

predefined tags, XML allows tags to be defined by the developer, rather like DATABASE records. The structure is defined in a DOCUMENT TYPE DEFINITION - what tags will be used, in what order they will be, and what tags are nested.

In this way, XML is not a true MARKUP LANGUAGE, but it allows new languages to be defined. The EXTENSIBLE LOG FORMAT language, for instance, defines a standard format for WEBLOG files. *See also* SCALABLE VECTOR GRAPHICS; WEB DESIGN; XHTML.

xmodem

An asynchronous file transfer protocol that facilitates error-free transmission of computer files through the telephone system.

XMS (eXtended Memory Specification)

A set of guidelines that standardize the method a programmer can use to access memory above 1024 KILOBYTES, which is the memory limit associated with Intel 8088 and 8086 microchips.

XON/XOFF

A method of communicating between MODEMS, whereby software controls the flow of data. In order that the two modems do not send data at the same time, one indicates that it wishes to send data by sending an XON code, and when it is finished it sends an XOFF code.

See also COMMUNICATIONS SETTINGS.

XSD (XML Schema Definition)

A way to describe and validate DATA in an XML environment. XSD was developed by the W3C and has

Zmodem

considerable advantages over earlier SCHEMA languages, such as DTD.

x-y plotter
A printer that creates a drawing by plotting x and y coordinates provided by the application program. This type of drawing is high precision and is commonly used for CAD drawings, architectural drawings and blueprints.

ymodem
An asynchronous file transfer protocol that is similar to xmodem but sends files in batches of 1024k as opposed to 128k.

zap
To delete or get rid of a program or file from a computer memory.

Zapf Dingbats
A set of decorative symbols developed by Herman Zapf, a German TYPEFACE designer.

z-axis
represents the third dimension in a three-dimensional graphic image. The third dimension represents depth.

zip
To COMPRESS files so that they utilize less space on a disk.

Zmodem
A fast and popular modem file transfer protocol.

zone

zone
A subgroup of networked computers in a LOCAL AREA NETWORK. Messages or ELECTRONIC MAIL can be addressed to everyone in the subgroup.

zoom
either to enlarge a window in order that it fills the screen or to enlarge or reduce the size of a page so that the full page can be seen on screen (*zoom out*) or the enlarged detail of the information in a smaller area can be seen (*zoom in*).

zoom box
A small box positioned at the edge of a screen window that is used to ZOOM a window.